When
Destinies
Are
Delivered

enjoy this.
Blessings to
you.

MAXWELL CRAPPS

When Destinies Are Delivered

Published by:
Christian International
177 Apostles Way
Santa Rosa Beach, FL 32459
www.christianinternational.com

In Partnership with:
A Book's Mind
PO Box 272847
Fort Collins, CO 80527
www.abooksmind.com

ISBN 978-1-939828-90-3

My long-time friend and colleague in ministry, Maxwell Crapps has written a stirring book that is difficult to put down. It matters little where you are in the scope of life, it will speak to you! Max's ability to communicate, along with the anointing of the Holy Spirit, causes this book to resonate with a "right now word" to all who read it. Go ahead and see for yourself. This book flows with nuggets of pure wisdom from the word of God and a man who lives it.

When Destinies Are Delivered, is destiny, being delivered. It is a product that comes from a tested vessel at a needy time. Maxwell's down-to-earth practical illustrations mixed with his experience inspire people to live on a new level with God. It is one of those books the Church was waiting for. Now that it's here, it needs to go home with you! When I read Max's new book, I was encouraged, and felt blessed to be his friend and honored to be his Pastor.

Johnny H. Moore
Lead Pastor, Family Worship Center
Cairo, Georgia

I have known Max since our days in Tulsa over 25 years ago and have been close friends with him ever since. He and his wife Lisa were a vital part of Abundant Life Fellowship for 12 years. Max was involved in many areas of our ministry and was a trusted Elder. We used His leadership abilities from the Helps Ministries to the Intercessory Prayer Team.

He has a heart for evangelism and is a gifted minister who walks out what he preaches. We were always enlightened and blessed by his candor in the pulpit and the humor that flowed in his messages. It is with highest regards that I can now recommend my friend and confidant to you as a gifted speaker and author.

Larry Millender
Pastor, Abundant Life Church
Tallahassee, Florida

In constant pursuit of God's best for himself and others is the way my husband and I have come to know Max the past 14 years. Being around him sharpens you, and his writings are a product of his surrendered life to God in prayer. He walks daily with a listening ear towards heaven and pens much of what he hears. His new book clears the air about the often misunderstood subject of destiny and will change, challenge and help you fulfill yours.

Stina Brockmann
Worship Leader and Teacher, His Glory to Nations
Tallahassee, Florida

In the words of my dear friend, Maxwell Crapps, "I'm gonna' be honest with ya'!" When Max first told me he was working on a book, I was a bit skeptical. I always enjoyed the home-spun humor he used so skillfully through the years to drive key points home while speaking. I just wasn't sure how it would translate into a written medium, or even if it could.

When I started reading the manuscript, success was the only word I needed to describe how he penned his heart and demeanor. I could almost hear him speaking as I read. I found myself not able to put it down until I had finished several chapters—not something I customarily do with my limited schedule.

When Destinies Are Delivered pulls and holds you in because there is so much you can relate to and glean from. This book, no doubt, will help each seeker gain a clearer understanding of how to naturally step into their destiny. Then it goes further by helping them bypass frustration and navigate around the obstacles in destiny's path. May each genuine seeker take this book, apply its timely principles and enjoy the fullness of what God has destined for them.

Charlie Daniels, M. Th.
Worship Pastor, Impact Church International
Concord, North Carolina

Maxwell delivers fresh insight with his new release When Destinies Are Delivered. It is full of practical wisdom and wit. As a wordsmith, Maxwell paints a picture of destiny that one can relate to. His universal language compels you to look again at what God has dealt your way until you see it.

Once you see it, the journey begins. His book is like a road map. It is filled with the multi-layered word, warning signs and experience to keep you on track. Your destiny is too precious to miss. This book will help you hit your target!

Shantae A. Charles
Pastor and Author of Church Love Novels
DC Metro Area

Max has a strong desire for people to enter into the Kingdom of God and not become lost in the crowd. He is gifted to help the parts of the body become grounded and find their place "in" the body. This book brings passed over scripture and experiences to light. It pictures real life incidents which prove all the young, middle and mature have a place in the Kingdom. If you, or know others, who need help finding their place, this book is a must. It points the way forward.

Ann Cope
Teacher of the Word, Prayer Warrior and C I Graduate
Thomasville, Georgia

Max is considered a son of New Generation Christian Center and has been part of this ministry for five years. His faithfulness to the Body of Christ is that of a warrior. He has a prophetic word today for this Joshua generation.

God has prepared him through his experiences and training to be able to meet the need of a generation that is crying in the wilderness. The anointing that is on his life to tear down and pull up is only a tip of what God is going to do in him, to him and through him.

New Generation has experienced the power of God through his preaching with signs and wonders following. We've seen what the Lord can do through this man of God as a preacher and now as an author. We "now" pray for his messages and books to keep coming.

Bishop Joe Frank Burns
New Generation Christian Center
Thomasville, Georgia

Dedication

This book is dedicated to the generations who scarce have time to put off what God has for them today. It is an investment into those who desire more out of life than the world has trained you to expect. It is for those willing to live outside the box of stale religion where the air is fresh with destiny. It is for the adventurous in spirit and those willing to take risks. It is for those willing to look again, at the hand, God has dealt them. I hope you are one of those. If you are, nothing compares to what God has waiting for you. This book was written to help you see it, experience it and deliver it. The day to mount up is now!

Special Thanks

I would like to give special thanks to the Lord of the harvest, Whom I believe has been waiting on me to produce this "particular" fruit for a while.

I would like to thank my Pastor Johnny Moore for the space, encouragement and trust he so willingly imparted to help me.

Many thanks go out to Amber Sutton for transcribing many of my notes and my daughter Claire D'Haeseleer for the remainder. Without their help, I'd still be months out. I also want to thank Claire for her editing and overall input.

Sincere thanks and appreciation to Loyd and Ann Cope, Edwin and Elaine Sanders, Linda Sullivan and all else who supplied prayer support.

And speaking of support, without reservations I owe much gratitude and thanks to my wife Lisa and Jon McHatton of Christian International Publishing. Jon urged me on, and Lisa gave me plenty of room at home. Both were a blessing.

In closing I would like to say thanks to my daughter Melissa (who thinks I can do anything) and all my family and friends who helped in any way. It takes a team and I'm glad you were part of it.

Table of Contents

Introduction

A verdict was reached long ago. The Judge of heaven and earth has sentenced you with a destiny. You are not on earth just to take up space. You have a life filled with appointments, and contributions to make. God sees you as valuable, and there is no reason to live below who you were destined to be. He wants justice carried out, and it matters little who says otherwise, unless you agree.

The cards of life aren't stacked against you, and it's impossible to relive yesterday. God has dealt you a winning hand! He desires for you to move beyond what has been, and move into what should be.

God has good plans for you, but many of you are looking at your futures like I was eyeing my cards one night long ago. We were playing seven-card poker with three cards wild, and my hand was looking great. I was anting up on every raise. The pot was full!

When show time came, I and the guy across from me had the best hands. However, I got confused looking at all those wild cards and money, and was about to fold to him. An older (and more experienced) friend next to me noticed my cards and dilemma and said, "Max, you better *look at your cards again*." I took another look and was thrilled that I did. I had the winning hand! Fireworks went off inside me. If my friend hadn't been looking out for me, I would have poured water on my own parade.

I can still see the dread on the other guy's face as I read aloud my winning hand. He was already counting my money and if looks could kill; my friend and I would've been six feet under. He was appalled at my friend's input, but too bad for him. I was dealt the winning hand! And if I had folded it, then I would have lost a bundle and had to leave the game. The lessons we learn in the natural realm should be applied in the spiritual.

I wasn't good at playing poker and haven't played for over thirty years, and would discourage anyone from going down that path. When I got saved, I realized gambling with what God had helped me earn wasn't wise. My money was too hard to make, and it was needed and promised elsewhere already.

The objective of the lesson learned is the principle to take away. Many of you just need to *look at your cards again.* The destiny that God has dealt you has some wild cards in it. You may have gotten confused in the shuffle of things, but you're holding more than you ever thought. Let Him help you see what's been dealt to you. It is no time to fold.

Failures can also confuse you about what God has dealt your way, but you're not to fold in life's game due to them either. Hebrews 12:1 tells us to lay aside the weights and sin that so easily beset us, so we can run with endurance the race that is set before us.

I've had a number of falls and my motto is: "When you fall, fall forward and get up quick, keep moving, for the crowd is coming and you could get trampled." Failures are only weights that need to be discarded. They can't bar you from your future. As you move forward in life, you will look back and thank God that many things didn't work out. That's a promise!

If it's been difficult to see the winning hand that God has blessed you with or get up from a fall, be encouraged—help is in your hands.

The serious must learn how to bond with God's will for their lives, and recognize how He has equipped them to succeed. You picked up the right book if you are ready.

Discerning the plans and purposes for our lives and learning how to navigate up-river with them are paramount. It is like mission impossible to attempt otherwise. Yes, the current will continue to push against our boats, but we will slip past much of the chaos and frustration that snag so many.

Having a destiny is one thing, delivering it is another. For instance, I'm sure Henry Ford knew he was destined to build and mass produce cars, and gifted with the ability. However, it took much effort, many failures, and many successes before his dream was rolling off an assembly line. He refused to allow his destiny of mass production to perish. He recognized his purpose alone would grind to a halt if his and others' abilities couldn't push it on. This made him a success, and put America on the road to their future.

What worked for him and many others will do the same for you. You can move steadily up-river with your dreams by grasping a few essentials. You've been given gifts, talents, and abilities your destiny requires for you to be successful. You must detect, develop, and utilize them for your dreams to come true. The purest motives alone will not succeed. With this perception, you can avoid the hit-and-miss method of many.

We all have natural and spiritual gifts that God expects us to function in life with, but we can lose sight of them. He recently shined His light on one in me which I had neglected, and I got up a changed man. New ideas, energy and desire exploded like fireworks as I set sail on this new course. Once you see your destiny, you can't live without it.

If you think you have waited too late to step into all or part of your call, think again. There are no expiration dates for those who dare to believe and are ready for their propellers of faith to spin.

Dry-docked destinies help no one. They only short circuit futures. Your boat must be lowered into the river of life to commence. It's time to get wet!

If you have questions about what God has gifted you with and how to handle it, do not feel like the Lone Ranger. Most of us are either with you, been there, or headed back. That only proves you are sincere. Our futures demand practical and spiritual choices as we move forward. Destiny is about communication, relationships and decisions.

This book was written to help the serious become the wise. We believe the insight herein will help you bond with, engage, and deliver your destiny. God intends for you to sail erect, dock at the right ports, and deliver the needed goods. He wants you to be a success in whatever vocation, ministry or position He's called you to.

In Matthew 5:16; Jesus said "Let your light shine before men, that they may see your good works and glorify your Father in heaven." When we shine (glisten, glow and stand out) in our callings, it has an effect on others.

When you deliver destiny, you become a distributor of God's supernatural plans and power. You not only witness, but often become a participant in changing the lives of many. Because of what's inside of you, dreams come true.

Friend, be assured you have valuable cargo, and people are waiting at the docks of life for you. Whether it's in your family, hometown, or miles away, we want to help you get there. As you follow others in this book as they read their wild cards and deliver their destinies, you will learn much of what it will take to deliver yours.

When the serious become the wise, destinies are realized. Your future is about to change if you are willing. If you want fireworks to go off in your life, I believe this God inspired message will help light the fuse.

Chapter One

Direction Is Vital

The pistol has been fired and the twenty first century race is on. Many of us are on board, or on the way. We are an intellectual, information-hungry lot, always looking for greener pastures to fulfill us. Better jobs, another town, new relationships, and a different church round out four fields of popular choice. Many fail to realize we are simply searching for the people and places that God has provided to help us engage with our destinies.

Yes, God has a place and people waiting just for you, and is well aware you need them. It is impossible for us to carry out the will of God in our lives alone. When others are helping us, they are delivering part of their destinies as well. It pays tremendous dividends to be at the right place with the right people, especially early on when we're most vulnerable.

***Many go out searching for platforms while
God is setting up their stage***

Being too restless and impatient to ask for directions, many speed away the wrong way. Much ambition with little guidance is a recipe to wonder. If that vital ingredient called direction is absent from our lives, much of our energy will be sapped away needlessly. We'll become less optimistic about our futures and even life itself. The mountains mock us when we're too tired to climb, and there is no enthusiasm in an empty tank.

Our enemy couldn't be happier than when we're burning rubber going nowhere. He enjoys watching us vigorously drain ourselves of our own resources. Then he will stand back blaming God for our fatigue. If we wear ourselves down before a race ever begins, where will our competitive edge be?

Moving is important, but direction is vital. Most who leave home without it are still searching for that well watered place God has for them. Some become discouraged and settle down wherever they can. They have a squatter's right mindset now. Camping there is illegal, but unless the Master comes and evicts them, camp they will.

Jesus had much to say about having an ear to hear, and nothing to say about putting our pedal to the medal. An ounce of prevention is worth far more than a pound of cure.

God isn't a busybody and doesn't wear a Rolex. However be assured He is full of peace and on time. That combination will work for us too. When we trust His calendar we enter His time zone. Ours is too busy any way. Religion has taught us to accomplish something quick. Our flesh agrees and says, "Yes, I need some gratification, let's go now." Jesus was never in a hurry.

He commissioned His disciples and us, to go into the world with the Gospel. He also told us to wait on the Holy Spirit before departing. Too many are leaving their Jerusalem and their place of prepping without Him and His guidance. Being commissioned is one thing; being prepared is another.

Wisdom is better than weapons of war... —Ecclesiastes 9:18

We are living in accelerated times unequaled in history, so attention to truth is a prized asset. Wisdom is essential to obtain and be our constant companion in this mobile age where mistakes are so costly. There is more movement in our world at present than all previous times combined. If we're not on a road trip, boarding a plane, or driving our daily routes, we're logged onto the Internet traveling places our incomes can't take us. We have tablets, smartphones, and apps galore. Just recently I added tiles to my transportation portfolio. We are a people on the move. Wisdom will keep you on course and away from needless wars.

A few tips can save needless trips. Point number one is—nobody needs to move with speed twenty-four-seven. If you do, you will miss some turns. The problem is most will be like those costly exits we miss on the interstate. God only knows how far we will have to go before we can turn around and head back to where we missed it. Our resources and fuel are too valuable to waste!

> ## There is no app to tap to keep us on course with our destiny

There is no app to tap to keep us on course with our destiny. If there was, hungry buyers with cash in hand, would clean the shelves daily. We'll gladly pay to have things quick and our way.

It may take more time up front to hear your Teacher, but the truth will set you free from many mistakes. I have learned from experience that moving is important, but directions are vital. I have also proved that a few good ones are far superior to many bad ones.

When traveling with assumption instead of good information, you can always depend on getting there late. I will humble myself at this time in order to help you bypass some of the pain I've endured. This is strictly for your benefit, so enjoy it.

My First West Goose Creek Outing

West Goose Creek Bay is somewhere hidden in the jagged coastline of Florida in Wakulla County. You really need a guide to get there. It is where West Goose Creek empties into the Gulf of Mexico. I heard my mother, aunt, and uncle speak about it many times growing up, and wanted to see this place they spoke of so fondly. It sounded like one of those hidden treasures most knew little about. History repeats itself, so maybe the next generation could cash in on this deal.

Due to its location and the condition of my car back then, I mentioned my desire to go with them if they ever went back. When I was in my early twenties the opportunity came and I seized it. There was room in the back seat of my Uncle Willie Mac's big Oldsmobile, so my wife, little daughter, and I were invited to go.

When he opened his trunk for us to load our chairs, it was quite shocking. He had fish cookers, fry pans, cooking oil, and anything else you could possibly need for a cookout. This man was prepared, and we were in for a treat. West Goose Creek, ready or not, here we come.

We sat in that huge backseat and listened to our elders talk and laugh about the good ole days. We could add very little to their conversations, so just took it all in. It was quite entertaining.

Upon arrival it was evident why they had spoken so highly of this place. There was no introduction to this campsite at all. It was like an action movie rolling the time you set in your chair. There were no previews, commercials, or long-winded rules to endure.

When we rounded the final bend and entered the small cove, it literally pulled you out of one world and cast you into another. After traveling through so much wilderness to get there, the activity woke us up like a five-a.m. alarm clock.

The local fishermen were already in the water holding up nets that were being released to them out of the back of small boats. They were forming half circles it seemed with their nets. People on the beach were pointing here and there in the water and shouting "here they come" or "there's a ripple to your right."

I saw none of what their sharp eyes caught, but was in awe of how everybody was involved.

You could tell they expected to catch quite a haul. People in battered shelters without walls were preparing their gear to clean the catch to be. The old tables that had been used for years were being pulled and positioned to be used again.

No wonder my mother and her clan enjoyed coming here. It was a total natural getaway. They were suspended from their agricultural life and exposed to a completely different way of living. That small beachhead of activity erased their problems and lifted their spirits. Mingling with the gulf people and listening to their stories only spiced it up more.

It was quite a treat to watch the local fishers cast off shore and wade out into the ocean. To witness these canny professionals scan the water with squinting eyes for that special effect a school of mullet created was intriguing. When they spotted their next paycheck, they would surround that group. At the right time their nets would be lowered, and they seldom came up empty. What they caught was pulled up to shore only a few feet away from the crowd. You felt involved!

The fish were separated and put in wash tubs, and sold immediately by their wives or partners. Each party had people to clean what you purchased. Buyers were plentiful that day as the weather was cool and perfect for a fish fry.

I'm well aware that some of you readers have never eaten fresh fried mullet. Others of you are saying "Uh, we only use them for bait food." If so, all I can say is, you've missed out on some fine eating. Fresh medium-sized mullet fried hot and crispy is hard to beat. If their red roe is in season, caviar of the South is on the menu too.

We bought our fish, fried it, and kept enjoying the show as we dined in the open air theater. It doesn't get much better than this. We had a great time.

My Second Trip to West Goose Creek

Years later, someone in our church came up with the idea for a West Goose Creek fish fry. My ears perked up immediately! I remembered the wonderful time we had previously and cast my vote to go. I had been there before so, "Yes, I can lead a couple of cars." We planned the trip and off we went.

> I RODE IN THE BACKSEAT BEFORE SO DIDN'T REMEMBER ALL THE TURNS BUT ASSUMED I WOULD.

I rode in the backseat before so didn't remember all the turns but assumed I would. The first half of trip went perfect. The second went south quick, and nothing looked familiar. My pride was in a vise and I prayed, "Please help me Lord." If He answered, I was too frustrated to hear. So I drove on and begged the landscape to awaken my memory. It never did.

We got so lost, went miles out of the way, and had several close encounters with each other. I was humiliated, and began asking directions from every human we saw. Problem was, not too many people were around that day, and what were gave pitiful directions.

After no small stir, we turned around and back-tracked for miles. I lost my leadership position, but fortunately, we finally came upon a guy that was able to help us. We followed his advice, and thank God, he was right. When we arrived at West Goose Creek Bay, I wanted to lock the doors and stay in the car. But due to all the heat on me, I had to get out and become their appetizer. I'd been there before.

You can learn two valuable lessons at my expense here. Just because you went somewhere as a passenger doesn't mean you're capable to lead others there. And just because a place was a hit once, there's never a guarantee it will be a success again. Too often we expect the same old results from the same old places, and not even sure how to get there. There are many West Goose Creeks out there waiting to break you from assuming and to crush you, too. I speak from experience; it was painful.

A third nugget of truth can also be dug out of my journey. When we embark on a trip for God or man, it is imperative to know whether it is north, south, east or west. God can better control His traffic when we give Him something to work with. I've found out that late is better than never. And If I don't hear "well done," I must hear "you tried."

There is wiggle room for error with God. However, the more we grow the less we can expect. If we miss a turn, God will do His part to get us rerouted. Signs will be posted, people will be positioned, and books will be given. He never gives up on us!

He has used some odd measures to keep some of us on course. A few have caused me to whine, resent Him, and blame half of Georgia for my problems. The truth is that most were alternative methods I forced Him to use to guide me into my future.

The Lord God will use a diverse group of people to keep you flowing with destiny too. I've gone through trials with unusual people, but profited from it. God sent a raven and not a dove to feed Elijah. Church folks aren't the only ones God will use to help, shape, or test you.

I had scores of opportunities to quit, but took none to heart. I knew my day was coming and kept running after God. Looking back I laugh at many of the sagas that almost took me out. I failed miserably often, but got back up and went again. What else is there to do, but go on with God?

My flight in life has been and still is, full of upgrades because I stayed on board with my destiny. It led me places I didn't understand at the time, but I didn't bail out.

Not every turn looked appealing, and I admit to refusing a few on the first pass. Fortunately, God has some equipment that will help us all become better navigators. There are those things you put in a horse's mouth called bits, and they are attached to a thing called a bridle. He carries my size in stock! I must confess they were a bit painful, but they greatly improved my turning technics. My listening skills have developed tremendously.

Unless we hear which way to go, what direction do we take?

Unless we hear where to go, what is our destination?

His direction is vital for you to move with your destiny and arrive on time at your place. Then you can step out and meet your party with all your resources.

Chapter Two

Destiny Knocks

"This is a good place for delivery." I was shocked! But without question, I heard the voice of God. To be honest, it wasn't even close to what I wanted to hear. Experience had taught me a few words from Him could mean a few years. I didn't plan to stay there that long. Maybe He was speaking to someone else in the church? A quick survey proved I was all alone.

"Lord, You have got to be kidding me! This church is in my hometown and the Bible is crystal clear about such places. I just want to keep a low profile here and prepare for delivery elsewhere. Plus, my wife Lisa already resents even being in Cairo, Georgia."

His seven words caused me discomfort even though I was in the midst of prayer. My defenses rose quickly! If Nazareth was offended by their hometown Jesus, where did that leave me?

I didn't have a clue where the Lord was going with that statement. I just knew I didn't want to go there. Plus there was no
urgent message inside to deliver anyway.

The sanctuary became quiet and I humbly knew it was time
to zip my lips. Why was I complaining anyway? This could be
the knock of destiny I had been waiting for. Was I arguing with
it now that it had sounded?

I knew complaining was a ball and chain. It holds us back
from hearing what will move us forward. When God became silent I knew I had overplayed my hand. Opportunity was knocking, and how easy it is to deny destiny when our taste buds are
offended in the least.

Destiny knocks. It doesn't kick the door open and super-glue
itself to you like many think. It presents itself, and we either
accept or reject it. I had become idle for the first time in a long
time and was enjoying it, but God had come with a ticket to
ride. I want everything He has for me and quickly discerned the
next was being offered. It was up to me to get on board or give
up my seat to another. This was an invitation to venture out and
experience the mores of God. Was I going to talk myself out of
it? Not hardly.

My excuses held little weight so I let them evaporate like
money at the mall. When the Lord spoke to me I failed to grasp
it all immediately, but I'm thankful I took the time and listened
to the rest of the story.

Believe me, I never claimed to be the sharpest knife in the
drawer, but a knife I am. I know God spoke to me. Even though
Moses saw a burning bush and Gideon saw an angel, the fact

remains, I heard a word from the same God they did. We read in the Bible where both of them put up a stellar defense before responding to God's knock. I was guilty of the same.

> WE ALL HAVE TO MAKE CAMP-BREAKING DECISIONS AT CERTAIN POINTS IN LIFE TO ADVANCE WITH DESTINY. I WAS THERE.

We all seem to, as my Dad used to say, "pull back" when God introduces the new. Even though we may have the stench of boredom and the taste of victory be foreign in our camps, many still have the mind to stay behind.

Leaving old mindsets and routines for an open door of opportunity requires a bold decision. But it's like playing a wild card, it can pay huge dividends. It can lift us out of our past and transfer us into our future. More may fall on our shoulders, but that is expected. What is life without challenge and some surprises? Faith will always arise when we are willing to press on. We all have to make camp-breaking decisions at certain points in life to advance with destiny. I was there.

Can two walk together, unless they are agreed?—Amos 3:3

I knew from experience if we are to walk forward with God's written or spoken word, we must agree with it first.

"Ok Lord, I may not feel anything moving inside, but that doesn't move me anymore. Let the records show, and let whoever needs to hear listen up, I agree with You! This is a good place for me to deliver something. Count me in. Now, what is it I am supposed to deliver here?"

I saw no lightning and heard no thunder. No rushing wind came in. But more importantly, He was talking again. His answer was conversational-like and to the point. The Lord spoke clearly to me by His Spirit, "You are to deliver a book here."

Now these seven words were more to my liking. My taste buds of destiny came alive. I sprang from the altar to grab my notebook. As He spoke, I furiously wrote. He said I had been called to write, but had ignored the gift. I had been too busy and hadn't thought it to be a priority. He also said I had experienced birth pangs of writing from time to time, but had never gone into delivery. It seemed I was satisfied just to feel a pang ever once in a while. His arrows of truth were a bit humbling.

Furthermore, He explained, "I have arranged this time and place for a transition. You're not an Elder, leader, or preacher here." He closed with three points. One, I had been pulled from projects to give birth to purpose. Two, it was now time for that baby to be delivered. Three, hometown or not, Cairo was my Bethlehem for now.

"How could I have been so blind? Now I had the time. The Lord knocked on my door that day with more of my destiny in

His hand. He was more concerned about my future than I was. His plans made mine look like unwanted company!"

"For I know the plans I have for you," says the Lord. "They are plans for good and not for disaster, to give you a future and a hope."—[NLT] Jeremiah 29:11

There are several definitions for destiny, but I prefer the one my Pastor Johnny Moore uses: an appointment by divine decree. Our destiny is God's path and plans for our lives, for only He knows what our potential is.

> ## OUR DESTINY IS GOD'S PATH
> ### AND PLANS FOR OUR LIVES.

You have untapped resources inside you that God wants brought out, developed, and utilized too. It may get a little wild at times, but it is part of your destiny. Whatever He's appointed you to, He's anointed you for.

In 11 Peter 3:9 the Bible plainly states that God is not willing that any should perish, and is inviting all to come to Him. It is also evident by the previous scripture, and many more in His word, that He has much more for us after the great gift of salvation. It is wonderful to know that our heavenly Father is not willing for us to perish in hell or perish in purpose.

Life without purpose is like a bird without wings. It is a strange looking creature and can never function as it was designed to. Purpose is a vital part of life. It fuels the fires of destiny, and help keeps our dreams alive. It gives life meaning!

God's plans and purposes for us are far superior to ours, but many fail to recognize them due to being hooked on theirs or others'. Too often we are just too busy to listen, and pay the piper for it.

I have chased trouble down with my plans before, and truth is, caught it. We've probably all caught a few things we wished had outrun us. It pays to go with the higher plan.

I knew the gift of writing was in me, and had written a few articles for the local paper, and many unpublished pieces, but was too busy to pursue writing books.

I missed God numerous times. Thankfully, He said in Isaiah 1:19: "If you are willing and obedient, you shall eat the good of the land." I am now both and challenge you to be the same with what God speaks to you about.

Gazing around the sanctuary the fireworks went off. God did not miss it. This was truly a good place to deliver a book. Destiny had knocked on my door. It was my time to go in labor. This was my Bethlehem for now, and I began to deliver.

Try to position yourself in an atmosphere to hear from God or create one, and sooner or later, you will hear Him knocking on your door. However, keep in mind that God doesn't require an invitation. He can show up at any time! Our attention is what He is after, and many times we are more willing to hear in a desert place than an oasis. The Lord has multiple ways to get our attention and will use whatever works best whenever the time is right. His desire is to speak into our lives wherever we are and help us move forward with His will. He will use His word, a preacher, a book, or even a bush to do either or both. When something is burning around us, we have a responsibility to give it our attention. The need is compounded when we're in a desert place, so it pays to be extra observant there. Moses was, and taught us all a valuable lesson.

Now Moses was tending the flock of Jethro his father-in-law, the priest of Midian. And he led the flock to the back of the desert, and came to Horeb, the mountain of God. And the Angel of the Lord appeared to him in a flame of fire from the midst of a bush. So he looked, and behold, the bush was burning with fire, but the bush was not consumed. —Exodus 3:1-2

God found Moses on the backside of nowhere. Do you know where that place is? "Yes," many of you are saying, "That's my address!"

> IT MAKES NO DIFFERENCE TO THE ANGEL OF THE LORD WHERE YOU LIVE.

That may be true but it makes no difference to the Angel of the Lord where you live. He created this world and us in it. He knows every nook and cranny on earth, and is aware of where we like to hide when we get out of stride. Like many of us, Moses knew he was called to be a deliverer. But also like many of us, he was hiding from his past.

Forty years ago, he perceived God chose him to lead his Hebrew brothers out of bondage from Egypt. The Palace life had spoiled him though. He was accustomed to getting his way without waiting. He had seen an Egyptian beating a Hebrew brother one day and took things into his own hands. That Egyptian never beat anybody again! Next day he was inspecting the congregation again, and two of his brothers were fighting. "Now what's wrong with these two?" Moses wondered.

He asked the one in the wrong why he was hitting his brother. Although Moses was aware of his destiny, the fighting brother wasn't. "Who made you to be a judge over us?" he asked angrily. "Do you intend to kill me as you killed the Egyptian?" The word had gotten out. Moses had murdered an Egyptian.

King Pharaoh had watched his daughter raise Moses in his Palace, and knew his descent. The boy had shown remarkable wisdom and could speak with the best even though he was an Israelite. None of that mattered now. He had struck down one of his. He had to pay with his life. Moses was well aware of the law and had only two choices. He could stay and lose his head, or run and find a different bed.

Like any of us would do in such a knotted position, he loosened himself from Pharaoh's Palace quickly. He became a pretty good long-distance runner overnight, and ran all the way to the land of Midian.

Through a series of events he met the Priest of Midian and married one of his daughters. Her name was Zipporah and she bore him a son he called Gershom, which literally meant, a stranger there.

Of course, he had to change occupations after his flight from Egypt. Sheep herding wasn't so bad once he got used to their bleating, and plus he could keep his head doing it.

Moses hadn't heard too much from God in forty full years. He didn't really miss the excitement of his old Palace life, but the call to lead his brothers from bondage haunted him. Regretfully he thought how little prepared he was when the Lord called him, and He never said now either. Herding sheep had built in him the patience Noah must have possessed when he built the ark. Moses often asked himself, "Why did I react so swiftly and violently years ago? What was I thinking of?"

Forty years of sheepherding had about convinced Moses he had missed his opportunity and the desert was his home. He contemplates going back to Egypt in his thoughts and dreams only. He wondered how his people were surviving under Pharaoh's brutal hand.

Moses regretted all the pride he attained in the Palace and how it had partnered with his anger. They prompted a terrible mistake! His impatient actions had severe consequences. At times he resented the man he killed.

> FORTY YEARS OF SHEEPHERDING HAD ABOUT CONVINCED MOSES HE HAD MISSED HIS OPPORTUNITY AND THE DESERT WAS HIS HOME.

The bleating of the sheep interrupted and reminded him it was time to lead them to another pasture. He has learned they are a lot like people. They make a lot of noise and never seem to be satisfied. He led them to the backside of the desert where they could graze and be a little cooler. He was hoping for some relief from both types of heat.

When they reached Mt. Horeb, Moses saw this sight that he'd never seen before. Something was burning, and it seemed to be a bush. But why wasn't it being consumed, and what did this mean? He looked closer and it was a bush, on fire. That wasn't unusual in the desert, but it not being consumed was. Bushes were only kindling wood for a fire, and were consumed in a few minutes. The site ignited a fire of interest in Moses.

Then Moses said, "I will now turn aside and see this great sight, why the bush does not burn." So when the Lord saw that he turned aside to look, God called to him

from the midst of the bush and said, "Moses, Moses!"
And he said, "Here I am." —Exodus 3:3-4

Whenever you're in a desert or wilderness place you need to keep your eyes and ears open, especially for the unusual. Make it a priority. Giving attention to it could be your ticket out.When Moses turned aside to look at the burning bush, then God began to speak. I believe He called his name twice to alleviate all doubt and have his full attention. Then He went on and assured Moses that the covenant He had with Israel was still in effect and so was his destiny. His days in the desert were over.

He told Moses in verse five, "Do not draw near this place. Take your sandals off your feet, for the place you stand is holy ground."

Then the Lord informed Moses that He was the God of his father Abraham, and that He had seen how the Egyptians were oppressing His people.

He went on to say in verse eight, "So I have come down to deliver them out of the hand of the Egyptians."

He was ready to take action on behalf of His people and free them from bondage. Moses had gotten his desert degree in patience and was now prepared to be their leader.

"Come now, therefore, and I will send you to Pharaoh
that you may bring My people, the children of Israel,
out of Egypt." —Exodus 3:10

The time had fully come and Moses was ready to deliver his destiny. He heard the knock of destiny in the Palace and heard it speak from a bush in the desert forty years later. The call hadn't changed, but he had.

He took his place in history and delivered his destiny and delivered a nation from bondage. How odd would it sound if someone else had led Israel out of Egypt and through the Red Sea?

Moses was in a desert place, but he didn't stay there forever. He dialed into his true destiny by taking the time to turn aside to see what God was up to. That act opened the door for him to leave.

> HE DIALED INTO HIS TRUE DESTINY BY TAKING THE TIME TO TURN ASIDE TO SEE WHAT GOD WAS UP TO.

If you are in a wilderness place, do not file for homestead exemption. God doesn't plan for you to live there forever. Be willing to turn aside from your normal course of travels to see what's burning, and God may rekindle and refine your call.

When Moses turned aside from what he was doing, then God told him what to do. Destiny knocks in different ways. We may hear, sense, or see it, but it's essential we answer. That one decision makes all the difference.

Chapter Three

Prophetess Deborah had the Credentials

The Lord had heard the cries of His people and was ready to answer them. King Jabin of Canaan was wreaking havoc on the children of Israel. The time had come for God to call Lady Deborah to judge and lead His nation out of bondage.

It was very cruel times for the children of Israel in Judges 4:1-3. The Bible states repeatedly that God shows no partiality among people. Sin always has a price and this time it was costing His Israel dearly. They had practiced evil in the Lord's sight, and now were crying out for Him to deliver them. King Jabin of Canaan had nine hundred chariots of iron, and his army commander Sisera knew what they were for. He had been harshly oppressing the children of Israel with every one of them and Jabin's huge army. This had been going on for twenty long years.

> DESTINY WAS CALLING DEBORAH, BECAUSE
> SHE HAD THE GOD GIVEN CREDENTIALS TO
> JUDGE IN SUCH A TIME AS THIS.

For anyone who believes that a woman can't lead in times of difficulty and war should have a change of mind after this chapter.

And, ye masters, do the same things unto them, forbearing threatening: knowing that your Master also is in heaven; neither is there respect of persons with Him.—Ephesians 6:9 [KJV]

It would benefit everyone to acknowledge this verse didn't just drop out of the sky and fall in front of Ephesians 6:10, which is the introductory verse on how to be strong in the Lord and dress for war. God purposely led the author apostle Paul, to insert it there to remind us that we're all soldiers of equality in His army. He decides our rank. Does faith play a role in His decision? I believe it does, and will rest my case there.

Remember, these were extremely harsh and punishing days in Israel. However, destiny was calling Deborah, because she had the God given *credentials* to judge in such a time as this. She was a woman of no small power or influence.

"Now Deborah, a prophetess, the wife of Lapidoth, was judging Israel at that time."—Judges 4:4

God couldn't make it much simpler! She alone was judging Israel at that time! The last sentence in Judges 4:5 goes on to add "And the children of Israel came up to her for judgment."

Some may ask, "Why did God call a female to lead Israel in such oppressive times?" Well, let's go back to the Bible for a few answers. In (vs.3) the children of Israel were crying out to the Lord to deliver them. After reading all of Judges 4:1-24 it is clear God answered their prayers by installing Deborah to judge and deliver them.

Secondly, during twenty years of oppression no one (male or female) had been bold enough to mount an attack against Sisera. Deborah was. God knew she had the faith and the boldness to use it.

Then she sent and called for Barak the son of Abinoam from Kedesh in Naphtali, and said to him, "Has not the Lord God of Israel commanded, Go and deploy troops at Mount Tabor; take with you ten thousand men of the sons of Naphtali and of the sons of Zebulun; and against you I will deploy Sisera, the commander of Jabin's army, with his chariots and his multitude at the River Kishon; and I will deliver him into your hand?"—Judges 4:6-7

There was nothing weak about this lady. She didn't stutter when she called for Barak and told him what the Lord God of Israel had told her to tell him. She spoke boldly. Faith knows how to talk.

She told Barak exactly where to deploy, who to take with him, and where to get them from. Then she told him what God would do and how He would deliver Sisera into his hand when he obeyed. It was her job to hear from God and proceed! She took her calling seriously.

And Barak said to her, "If you will go with me, then I will go; but if you will not go with me, I will not go!"— Judges 4:8

Thirdly, Barak knew beyond a doubt if Deborah accompanied him to the battle, the presence of God would be with him. Victory would be a sure thing no matter the number of Jabin's chariots or men. Barak recognized the authority of God in Deborah and knew he could trust her. He didn't ask for or require any other man or woman to go with him.

So she said, "I will surely go with you..."—Judges 4:9

Fourthly, Israel needed somebody with a warrior's heart and ready to lead. Deborah filled both shoes. She arose and went with Barak. Destiny knows how to walk and lead.

> **God is no respecter of persons. Female or not, He chose it to be Deborah's time to shine!**

She told him exactly when the Lord went out before him, which was his cue to march. Barak then followed with his ten thousand men and the Lord routed Sisera and all his chariots and all his army.

Fifthly, God is no respecter of persons. Female or not, He chose it to be *Deborah's time to shine!* Judging was her destiny, deliverance was her call, and she delivered in style.

"For the eyes of the Lord run to and fro throughout the whole earth, to show Himself strong on behalf of those whose heart is loyal to Him..." —11 Chronicles 16:9

I fail to see gender or age was mentioned when the prophet Hanani spoke this message of warning from God to King Asa of Judah. Hearts that are *loyal to Him* is what the Bible says God is searching for. So He can show Himself strong on *their* behalf, whoever *they* may be!

Praise the Lord, all you Gentiles! Laud Him, all you peoples! For His merciful kindness is great toward us,

*and the truth of the Lord endures forever. Praise the
Lord! —Psalm 117:1-2*

*"But the word of the Lord endures forever." Now this
is the word which by the gospel was preached to you.—
1Peter 1:25*

It seems to me that, according to the Bible, God has no intentions of changing His mind about this issue or any others that
may perplex some. His word endures forever, and He searches
on today for *those* He can show Himself strong in.

Oh, I was about to forget! Did I mention a woman named
Jael, who was the *wife* of Heber, was the one who personally
took out commander Sisera by herself? It seemed to be part of
her destiny.

Both women had loyal hearts, and made strong deliveries on
their destinies. God used Barak and a host of other men in that
great victory, but Deborah and Jael stood out amongst them all.

Let it be known, God is not into playing favorites. He wants
to use you, and the credentials He has blessed you with. Every
destiny delivered promotes the Kingdom of God on earth.

Deborah refused to neglect her gift from God. As a prophetess judging Israel during a serious time of oppression, I'm sure
she had to stir up her gift often. She had to pray to God, talk to
herself and declare to her enemies how God had gifted her. You
will have to do the same under similar circumstances. However, by embracing her destiny, God showed Himself strong on
her behalf, and she delivered a nation from bondage. The Bible
leaves no doubt that a woman of God can be used mightily, even
in perilous times.

Chapter Four

Summoned to Destiny

Young David was summoned to destiny and it surprised everyone. Your summons to destiny may be a shocker too. Like many, he was completely overlooked by everyone around him. He was totally forgotten about when the prophet Samuel came to his family's house in search of a new king for Israel. Father Jesse didn't even consider calling his ruddy looking youngest from the sheep herd.

He proudly lined up his seven other sons to be inspected for the royal position and wondered which it would be. The prophet eyed Jesse's seven in 1 Samuel 16:6-10, but ran into a wall. All seven failed inspection. The Lord hadn't chosen any of them to be His king.

Thus Jesse made seven of his sons pass before Samuel. And Samuel said to Jesse, "The Lord has not chosen these."—1 Samuel 16:10

God had told the prophet in 1Samuel 16:1 to go to Jesse's house because He had provided Himself a king among his sons. The prophet had obeyed but seemed a bit stressed when all the prospects present were rejected. Then he wondered, "Does Jesse even know how many sons he has?"

And you can almost hear Jesse thinking, "The prophet missed it on Eliab. The only one left is David and he is a mere child, and a strange one at that. He only likes tending sheep, looking up to Heaven, and singing songs to the Lord. He's a musician, not a king to be."

Samuel's patience with Jesse and his seven sons was being tested. Something was missing! Irritated, he cut to the quick with Jesse.

And Samuel said to Jesse, "Are all the young men here?" Then he said, "There remains yet the youngest, and there he is, keeping the sheep." And Samuel said to Jesse, "Send and bring him. For we will not sit down till he comes here." —1 Samuel 16:11

With all hope dashed of his eldest and other favorites being chosen, what did Jesse have to lose? He sent for David, who was, of course, out tending the sheep. So it took a while for him to get there.

I find it rather odd that none of Jesse's other sons worked in the family business. They all seemed to be waiting around the house for some reason. I wonder what for? But since they enjoyed squandering time, they could wait until their little brother arrived from the pasture.

That would give them time to make up jokes about how the prophet missed it, and how he would call for a reinspection when kid brother appeared. "He will see us in a different light then," they thought.

Little did they know while they had been knocking around doing nothing, David had been knocking on the heart of God with his songs of praise. God was now only minutes away from summoning him to his destiny.

David entered the line-up wondering "what's going on?" and without hesitation, the Lord orders Samuel in the next verse: "Arise, anoint him; for this is the one."

The number seven represents completion and, sure enough, the seven brothers that were so used to just hanging out were completely left out.

> THE HIGHER THE SUMMONS IS, THE LONGER
> THE TRAINING USUALLY TAKES.

The boy heard the Lord approaching long before Samuel came with the anointing oil, but look what happened when the oil was poured over him.

Then Samuel took the horn of oil and anointed him in the midst of his brothers; and the Spirit of the Lord came upon David from that day forward.—1 Samuel 16:13

His family had to see it to believe it so the Lord gave them a front-row seat. The time would come when what they beheld would be of great value.

It took David quite a while to prepare for the royal position he was summoned and anointed for. The higher the summons is, the longer the training usually takes.

He had to prove he would lay his life on the line to protect his father's sheep before God could trust him with His children. There were some lions and bears he had to kill first. We will check back in on his progress later.

When you are summoned to destiny for a special position or purpose, it may surprise everyone around. Begin to prepare by being faithful where you are, because God has a way of calling people out of the shadows when He and they are ready. Your call may land you on center stage, but it may not be what you expected.

God is into diversity, and anyone who thinks He is normal is in for a shocker when they get to know Him. He will call the unexpected and equip them to do the impossible in front of many spectators.

Your Call may draw a Crowd

When you hear the rap-rap-rap of God at your ear gate, you can bet He's gone shopping just for you. The only thing you can be certain of is; whatever He's brought is different from anything you have. And so it was with Noah.

The wickedness of man had become so great in Noah's day that every intent and thought of man's heart was only evil. Man was on a wicked downward spiral of self-destruction.

God was grieved in His heart at what the people He had created and loved had become. Adam's sin in the garden had cut man to the core, and was about to expel him from more than just the Garden of Eden. It would take drastic measures for God to salvage the human race. He needed one just man to stand in the gap and willing to follow His orders and be mocked for a hundred years plus. One's destiny would require it.

But Noah found grace in the eyes of the Lord. This is the genealogy of Noah. Noah was just a man, perfect in his generations. Noah walked with God. And Noah begot three sons: Shem, Ham, and Japheth. The earth was also corrupt before God, and the earth was filled with violence. So God looked upon the earth, and indeed it was corrupt; for all flesh had corrupted their way on the earth. And God said to Noah, "The end of all flesh has come before Me, for the earth is filled with violence through them; and behold, I will destroy them with the earth. Make yourself an ark of gopher wood; make rooms in the ark, and cover it inside and outside with pitch (tar)..." Genesis 6:8-14

God went on and gave Noah the blueprints for the ark. It was to be 450 feet long, 75 feet wide, and 45 feet high with a window below the roof line and a door on the side. He was to build three decks inside: a lower, middle, and upper deck.

FULFILLING OUR DESTINIES HAS A DIRECT
EFFECT ON OUR CHILDREN.

By anybody's calculations, this is a giant of a boat. Keep in mind this ark would be one hundred and fifty feet longer than a football field. With little as they had to work with back then it would take you or me, with plenty of help a lifetime and then some to construct a boat of this caliber.

Fortunately the life expectancy in those days was several hundred years or more. Noah and his three sons and all of their wives could achieve this daunting project together. He and his family spent the next one hundred years plus building the ark that would save their lives. Of course, a certain number of the animals, birds, and everything that crept upon the earth sought safety in the ark too.

Thus Noah did; according to all that God commanded him, so he did.—Genesis 6:22

Notice how Noah followed God's instructions to the smallest detail. He did all that the Lord directed. His punch-list was punched out.

Fulfilling our destinies has a direct effect on our children. What might the next verse have read like if Noah has said no to the Lord?

Then the Lord said to Noah, "Come into the ark, you and all your household, because I have seen that you are righteous before Me in this generation."—Gensis 7:1

Where would Noah's wife, sons, and daughters-in-law have been if he had not said yes to the call of God on his life? I will tell you exactly where they would have been—strung out all around the mountains and meadows rotting with all the rest of the earth's dead. It's not pretty, but it's the truth.

God told him to build an ark because He was going to send a flood. What if Noah had refused and said, "Lord, it's never even rained and what's a flood? Do you realize the ridicule my family and I will endure? We will be mocked by everyone. Do You comprehend the enormity of what You're asking me to do? We will be the joke of the entire world, because it'll take us over a hundred years to complete the project. Word will get out, and people will come from all over to witness this peculiar project and mock us."

My one and only point is; people will typically mock anything new and what they fail to discern. This was against Noah's human understanding, but he refused to let his mind control his and his family's destiny.

Had he not stayed his course for a hundred years plus while he and his family was the joke of the world, I pose to you a question. Would we be here today? Had he not been willing to live with the animals in tight smelly quarters, would they be here with us? And excuse my boldness if this next question seems morbid. What if Noah had not been willing and obedient to leave the side door closed when he and his family heard the scratching and screams of those who mocked him when the waters began to rise?

Try to form a picture in your mind of the pandemonium that would have followed if he had made the mistake and opened that door. The ark's door would have been rushed by thousands. Chaos and murder would have been the norm till so many people inside capsized the ark and all was lost. Everybody knew it was the only way out, but time had lingered and caused all to doubt. Noah's sons would never have had the opportunity to re-populate the earth with God's family had that side door been opened.

There is one thing in life it pays to be fully aware of. It is absolutely irrelevant who mocks you as long as you are following God's instructions, and working His plan for your life. When the rain came, Noah didn't look so foolish then.

Chapter Five

Why all this Struggle?

Now Isaac pleaded with the Lord for his wife, because she was barren; and the Lord granted his plea, and Rebekah his wife conceived. But the children struggled together within her; and she said, "If all is well, why am I like this?" So she went to inquire of the Lord.
—Genesis 25:21-22

Nearly one hundred percent of people go through what Rebekah was questioning the Lord about. I sure have. We've pleaded and had others plead to God for us because we were barren in some area of our lives. Then like Rebekah, God would bless and conception would take place. Then things would begin to grow and move and need more space. That's when things start to annoy us and then some type of struggle begins.

I suppose Isaac had tried to comfort his wife by telling her something like, "Sweetheart, you are just pregnant and this is your first time. You will feel better soon, and the baby will be fine. Trust me, everything is well."

His answer to her problem was about the same as most male's and got about the same reaction. She fired back, "If all is well, why am I like this?" Isaac acted with much wisdom at that point and was absolutely silent. So she went to inquire of the Lord. She knew where to go for answers when her husband didn't have them and things were getting hectic.

And the Lord said to her: "Two nations are in your womb, Two peoples shall be separated from your body; One people shall be stronger than the other, And the older shall serve the younger." Genesis 25:23

Rebekah knew something was going on, and when her husband couldn't explain it, she wasted no time in going to God for the answer. How we could profit by following her example! The sooner we find out what's inside of us, the sooner we can calm down, flow with it, nourish it and deliver it, or them, in Rebekah's case.

No wonder Rebekah felt such a struggle in development! During her long awaited first pregnancy she had twins pushing and shoving one another inside of her. Normally, the first male that exited the womb got a double portion of his father's estate. Whether this was in their DNA or not, who is to say? However, they did seem to be aware of this even in the womb.

When Rebekah delivered her two sons, both were still struggling to be the first one out. The latter had a hold on the frontrunner's heel and trying to pull him back in it seemed. The attempt failed and Esau was born first and then Jacob.

So when her days were fulfilled for her to give birth, indeed there were twins in her womb. And the first came out red. He was like a hairy garment all over; so they called his name Esau. Afterward his brother came out, and his hand took hold of Esau's heel; so his name was called Jacob. Isaac was sixty years old when she bore them.—Genesis 25:24-26

When it's time for delivery, babies naturally start moving. They must get in the right position to be born. The same is so in the spirit realm. There is what I call a "positioning struggle" there also. When gifts, callings, and abilities are ready to come out of you to help deliver your destiny, it can be an irritable time. They begin to move about and can cause discomfort too. Like Rebekah, you can't see them, but they're clamoring to come out into the world. It's their time!

The Struggle Inside

There was a struggle taking place inside me. Like Rebekah, I was pregnant with more than I could see. I became irritable within myself, and it can happen to you too if it isn't already in progress. The gift of writing was struggling inside of me to come out. I was going through an uncomfortable transition. Life had been great a few weeks ago. "What's up now?" I thought.

I had enough smarts to refuse to play the blame game. I stayed my normal course of prayer, meditation in God's word, and encouraging myself to continue moving forward. I could tell it wasn't bothering anybody but me. All else seemed happy and oblivious to my condition.

> THE SOONER WE FIND OUT WHAT'S INSIDE OF US, THE SOONER WE CAN CALM DOWN, FLOW WITH IT, NOURISH IT, AND DELIVER IT.

The world hadn't changed, but I had. After a few weeks of wrestling with this issue, I realized this wasn't a passing thing. Something in me seemed to be out of order. My wife was gracious and gave me space, but after several weeks I had all the room I needed. Now I wanted an answer!

I'm not one to let a problem of mine rock on very long. Problems have a way of getting infected and spreading to others, and others have enough difficulties already. My philosophy is, "Whatever is going to happen by addressing an issue in my life, let it happen so I can either rejoice or get over it." So like Rebekah, this situation had gone on long enough. I needed revelation why I was like this, if all was well.

The Bible in James 4:3 explains to us that the main reason we fail to have is that we fail to ask with the right motives. My motive was right. I wanted to know what all the struggling in me was about so I could move on with God.

So like Rebekah I went and asked God, "Why do I feel so disconnected from everybody and everything I was close to just weeks ago? I've been praying more and studying Your word more in depth than ever, but yet it seems something is just not right. What is it?"

He was not hesitant to answer Rebekah and neither was He me. If you are going through some of the same, neither will He be with you. He let me know I had more inside of me than preaching and everything else I was doing. I didn't get the complete answer on the spot, but got what I needed to be content.

Days later, while at prayer in the church we had only been attending several weeks, He gave me the full answer. I was more prepared for it then, but still was taken back a bit as I explained in chapter two. He had called me to write books too, and that gift was struggling to get out and engage. Allowing God to deliver a gift that He birthed in you is somewhat like delivering a natural baby. You are uncomfortable for weeks and then it tends to take up much of your time for a season.

Remember, the sooner we find out what's inside of us, the sooner we can calm down, flow with it, nourish it, and deliver it. Then watch out, it could happen all over again. It is somewhat like having natural children.

It is only wisdom to look to God when you sense a struggle taking place inside you. An answer from Him can lift the anxiety and allow you to carry on with harmony. Then you can deliver that gift or let that hidden talent be exposed and used. I believe much of the anguish we often endure is simply because we either walk in denial or get a wrong answer and give up. Remember,

Rebekah did neither, she went to the Lord and got her assurance and carried on.

Many who were pregnant with gifts, callings, and abilities, but weren't aware of how to get through the struggling period, have suffered needlessly. Many in the midst of frustration became resentful when God wouldn't deliver them immediately. Some have even thought, "If this is what I get for serving God, somebody else can have it." However, we must remember that mothers go into delivery when the baby is ready to be born.

If you fail to see the big picture, call time-out and ask God about it. He is waiting to inform you of what's going on. The struggle is due from what's inside of you. There is more in there than you thought and it's growing, moving and getting in position to come out. The sooner you perceive the sooner you are relieved.

The Abrahamic covenant and the nation-to-be, Israel, both depended on Isaac and Rebekah to have a son. Jacob had to come! Remember in verse 21 how Isaac pleaded with the Lord for his wife because she was barren. He prayed for her to conceive for twenty long years. She wasn't the only reason for all those prayers. He knew future generations depended on him and Rebekah. As all are aware, our children and others are directly affected by our choices in the natural world. Do we think it is much different in the spiritual world? If so, I believe we deceive ourselves.

Sometimes God wants to know how strong our desire is to birth what He has for us. Who today is hungry enough to spend time in prayer for it like Isaac?

God only knows who is depending on you to deliver the gifts, promises, and callings you may be pregnant with. Present and future generations may deeply be affected by your decisions. Delivering what God has conceived in you is well worth the struggles you may go through. And it should embolden you that God never intended them to last forever. They're like tests and just part of the process of delivering your destiny.

I'm convinced that clarity of whatever may be struggling inside us will expel tension, bolster our faith and help with our deliveries.

Chapter Six

Launch Out

You may still believe stepping into destiny and delivering it is for others, but not for yourself. This could never be further from the truth. You always need to remember, God is no respecter of persons. That means you are not excluded. It doesn't matter what you've been taught or what people may say; Jesus has a future and a destiny with your name written all over it. He is just waiting on you to say "yes" to it.

And remember that the heavenly Father to whom you pray has no favorites...—1Peter 1:17 [NLT]

Our heavenly Father has no favorites, but understands some of us have to fish around a while in life and just get tired before we will listen. We can make it so complicated when it's so simple.

In Luke 5, the multitudes were pressing about Jesus to hear the Word of God. They recognized the truth. He was standing by the Lake of Gennesaret (Sea of Galilee) to give his audience room on its shores. So many people came that He was physically being pushed into the edge of the water.

He sees a floating platform is needed quick.

So it was, as the multitude pressed about Him to hear the word of God, that He stood by the Lake of Genn-nesaret, and saw two boats standing by the lake; but the fishermen had gone from them and were washing their nets. Then He got into one of the boats, which was Simon's, and asked him to put out a little from the land. And He sat down and taught the multitudes from the boat.—Luke 5:1-3

Sometimes Jesus (the living Word of God) will just step into your boat without knocking, and it would be wise to listen when He does. When He comes in that close, He has something for you. You may be so overworked and frustrated like Peter was that it's been very difficult to hear His voice, but He is concerned about you.

If you fail to hear Him knock the first time, the Lord has a way of showing up again when you are ready to listen. He will return to you at that special time. It could even be at your workplace or business.

When He had stopped speaking, He said to Simon, "Launch out into the deep and let down your nets for a catch." But Simon answered and said to Him, "Master, we have toiled all night and caught nothing; nevertheless at Your word I will let down the net."—Luke 5:4-5

Jesus' teaching to a tired Simon caused just enough hope to spring up to allow him to let go of last night's failure. He hears "Launch out!" loud and clear. His flesh wants to go home but the gaze of Jesus' eyes will not leave him alone. That command produced a bit of unexplainable faith in Peter too.

> SOMETIMES, JUST A LITTLE FAITH WITH SOME ACTION WILL CHANGE EVERYTHING.

Destiny is now knocking, but it's different from anything he's ever heard. Who in the world goes fishing in the day when the fish can see your boat a mile away? The evening is the best time to fish, but Peter had heard the Word. His ice chest was empty; he was tired of fishing, and tired of facing his wife empty handed. He was run-down and fed-up.

"Nevertheless," leaves his lips, and he wasn't sure where it came from. Something inside answered the knock. Listen to his follow up again: "At Your word I will let down the net." In other words, he was saying, "I will shove my boat back out to sea when I want to go home. I will let down my net when I should lie down and rest. I want this multitude to understand this simply is not the way you fish. I don't agree with it, but I'm going to do it anyway, because You said to. And if I come back empty handed, it's Your fault. You are the One they will laugh at, not me. I'm just obeying Your orders."

And when they had done this, they caught a great deal of fish, and their net was breaking.—Luke 5:6

Sometimes, just a little faith with some action will change everything. Peter was hesitant to obey this contrary command of Jesus, and many of us find ourselves in the same boat. We protect ourselves as much as possible. It's what we're used to. The fear of failure, keep many in shallow water or at the docks.

However, Peter wasn't overlooked because of his protectionist mindset. Jesus just flushed it out of him with a great catch of fish.

Peter's actions gave Jesus the green light for a miracle to take place. He spoke his doubt, but pushed out into the deep. His fish were there! Our actions speak louder than our words, and God can use them in a very positive way.

Peter's net was breaking and so was his previous mindset about fishing and everything else. When the great number of fish began to break his net, he excitingly remembered what Jesus told him. He said to "Launch out into the deep and let down your nets for a catch." Peter is bouncing all over his boat. "What if I had brought more nets like He said?" I was just trying to protect myself, plus Him, and look at the mess I'm in. My one net is breaking."

I can see Jesus laughing now! He's laughed at me before when I played my protectionist hand and was caught off guard with His results. If God has wrinkles, it's from laughing at us.

Peter was in a frenzy. His net just became a fish magnet and he needed his partners to come quickly and help him land this net breaking miracle.

So they signaled their partners in the other boat to come and help them. And they came and filled both the boats, so that they began to sink.— Luke 5:7

His partners came making more noise than fifty boats, but it didn't bother the fish one bit. They were destined to fill the boats of this rowdy bunch. They just kept coming. Both boats were beginning to sink now with fish. Everyone was thinking the same regretful thought. "What if we had brought more boats!" Who knows where all this would have ended if they had.

When Simon Peter saw it, he fell down at Jesus' knees, saying, "Depart from me, for I am a sinful man, O Lord!"—Luke 5:8

When Peter saw Jesus for who He was, he saw himself for who he was. If you've never seen who Jesus really is, slow down here and take a good look.

Simon Peter, amazed by His goodness and holiness, said in essence, "Jesus, You don't need to be around such a sinful person such as myself." But Jesus has only begun to knock on this bunch of roughneck fishermen.

For he and all who were with him were astonished at the catch of fish which they had taken; and so also were James and John, the sons of Zebedee, who were partners with Simon. And Jesus said to Simon, "Do not be afraid. From now on you will catch men."—Luke 5:9-10

With that great catch of fish, He knocked on the door of Simon Peter's partners too. James and John were known as the sons of Zebedee, or better known as the "Sons of Thunder." They proudly lived up to the family tradition. They made much uproar and clamor and were good at backing up their noise with action.

If you're not a Christian by now, let me tell you the truth: you don't have any idea what you're missing. It's the greatest life imaginable. I'm high on it as I write! I can hardly contain myself. Do you really think God can handle the notoriously loud and bodacious Sons of Thunder and then have trouble with you? I challenge you to launch and see.

What Peter said was true for everyone, and Jesus' reply was also. He doesn't drive anyone away or hang around a select few. He pulled *closer* to Simon by drafting him into His service and wants to do the same with you. God has an extreme sense of humor, and is not anywhere close to being religious (like the hard-hearted Pharisees in the Gospels). He lifts people up, even the unlikely.

So when they had brought their boats to land, they forsook all and followed Him. —Luke 5:11

Here's another thing to ponder. What if Peter had not acted that day with his nevertheless attitude of faith? Would the wild Sons of Thunder have seen what they needed to see, to become Sons of God? Would they have taken their places in history as two of the twelve apostles that walked, witnessed, and worked miracles alongside Jesus? Would they have been in the upper room on the day of Pentecost, and then pillars in the early church?

One man, woman, or child answering the knock of destiny has far reaching effects. You may have been fishing around in life till now and are tired, but the Master sees where you are. He is stepping into your boat now because it is that precise time when you're ready to listen. Hear him, and act on His word to you. Push yourself out with a nevertheless attitude if you must, but launch out where Jesus directs you nonetheless.

He has more for you to catch than you ever dreamed possible. It will take more than just that one net you're accustomed to.

Chapter Seven

Gates Have Timers

Only two men of warrior status survived through Israel's 40 years of wandering in the wilderness. These two alone entered the Promised Land that God delivered them out of Egyptian bondage to inherit. In forty years these two had watched over five hundred thousand men of warrior status (20 years or older) die wandering in the wilderness when they could've been living in their promised land. Rebellion and a bad report by ten spies cost a grueling forty years and thousands to die.

God's little nation Israel had been in bondage four hundred years in Egypt. He had called Moses to lead them out and performed ten mighty miracles to convince King Pharaoh to let His people go. Destiny was at work.

After Pharaoh finally let the children of God leave, he had a change of heart. His workforce without wages had just left. Who would build his statues, palaces, and pyramids now? He called out to his generals to pursue, capture, and bring his free workforce back into bondage. Pharaoh himself joined all his charioteers and army in chasing down the Israelites. They caught up with them camped by the Red Sea. Pharaoh thought he had corrected his mistake. They would be easy pickings here, for there wasn't anywhere for them to go. He had them again and they would pay dearly for leaving.

But all of a sudden a cloud stood between the children of God and Pharaoh's army. On Pharaoh's side it was dark and they couldn't see a thing. It paralyzed them. On Israel's side it gave them light at night. Had Pharaoh forgotten about Israel's wonder working God so soon? The Red Sea wouldn't stand in the way of Israel's destiny. It was part of it!

Then Moses stretched out his hand over the sea; and the Lord caused the sea to go back by a strong east wind all that night, and made the sea into dry land, and the waters were divided.—Exodus 14:21

I can only imagine the disappointment and humiliation that the cloud caused in Pharaoh's camp. Somehow it wasn't enough to discourage them to tuck tail and run. It must have caused more determination in Pharaoh and angered him to pursue at all cost. Pride goes before a fall.

So the children of Israel went into the midst of the sea on the dry ground, and the waters were a wall to them on their right hand and on their left.—Exodus 14:22

If Pharaoh's army had one lick of sense they would have deserted that day. Did the cloud relieve them of their senses or did Pharaoh threaten to reduce them to making pyramids? It worked if he did. Seems to me it would have been a perfect time to volunteer to make and lay bricks.

And the Egyptians pursued and went after them into the midst of the sea, all Pharaoh's horses, his chariots, and his horsemen.—Exodus 14:23

The same waters that stood up for Israel came down on the Egyptians. Not one made it out alive. Pharaoh had no choice now. He had to cut his losses and sell his horse feed before it went bad, and start over. The Bible tells us that whoever digs a hole for someone to fall into, will fall into it themselves. I refuse to believe Pharaoh ever got out of the one he dug for Israel.

A year had passed and Israel was approaching their destined promised land. There hadn't been any lack of complaining along the way either. They had tested God's and Moses' patience to the limit at times. Some were tried and convicted on the spot for their rebellion and sin. Hundreds of them had refused to adhere to God's ways and were no longer around. In spite of all that and more, God and Moses had the majority of them positioned to enter their land that was flowing with milk and honey. This was the place God destined them to have.

And the Lord spoke to Moses saying, "Send men to spy out the land of Canaan, which I am giving to the children of Israel; from each tribe of their fathers you shall send a man, every one a leader among them."—Numbers 13:1-2

A leader from each of the twelve tribes of Israel was chosen to spy out their land of destiny. These rugged men of valor were hand-picked to explore and spy out a beautiful but treacherous land filled with seven strong enemy nations. All twelve had to be physically fit, daring, and adventurous to say yes to this call. Life had schooled them about "sudden death" long before football added it to break a tie in the 20th Century.

These twelve stand-outs had seen the hand of God move on their behalf and were eager to launch on the covert operation. Off they went, and what a scene they beheld. It was a lot like the abundant life that Jesus said He came for us to have in John 10:10. It had majestic mountains, lush valleys, and plains in between. It was decorated with springs and had an oasis here and there. All in all, it flowed with milk and honey. It was perfect for raising livestock and farming.

This place was the closest thing to Eden they'd ever seen. Egypt with its Nile could not even hold a light to this land. Who ever saw a cluster of grapes so large that it had to be carried on a pole atop the shoulders of two strong men? And God had already said He was giving them this place. Wow, what a turnaround! Previously, there was no future in sight. Now things are looking rather bright.

After forty days, the troops returned to Moses. The people were excited to no end. Everyone wanted to know what it was like. "Truly it was a dream land," the spies said. And truly it was. Whatever they needed, it had. The place flowed with provision and possibilities and had the most beautiful landscape you could ever imagine. It was totally different from the dry flat place they just left. The people were ecstatic and emotions reached the sky. The branch of grapes they cut down spoke volumes.

Then it happened. Ten live arrows of doubt shot forth from the bow of rebellion punctured the faith of a nation.

But the men who had gone up with him (Caleb) said, "We are not able to go up against the people, for they are stronger than we." —Numbers 13:31

With their mouths of doubt, they drained a nation's hope with one simultaneous piercing assessment of their destined place. A spiked jury gave the wrong verdict! Ten of the twelve had already forgotten about their God who opened the Red Sea and provided for them since leaving Egypt. Their opponent's size filled their eyes, and human reason materialized.

Yes—yes, it's great to see, but in this land giants there be. We looked at them as they looked at us and we ten agreed; we'll be trampled into dust. This ten finger verdict of man left God completely out of their deliberation. The people began to cry, and moaned all night long.

It was crucial for them to remember that the One who provided a way through the Sea, didn't intend for the enemy to reign where they should be.

> FEARING MAN OR OBSTACLES WILL
> CAUSE YOU TO CAST YOUR OPINION
> AND VOTE YOURSELF OUT OF GOD'S
> TIMING AND YOUR DESTINY.

Two of the twelve had no problem with their memories that day. Those rose up with a different spirit and point of view. They quieted the people and spoke.

But Joshua the son of Nun and Caleb the son of Jephunneh, who were among those who had spied out the land, tore their clothes; and they spoke to all the congregation of the children of Israel, saying: "The land we passed through to spy out is an exceedingly good land. "If the Lord delights in us, then He will bring us into this land and give it to us, a land which flows with milk and honey. Only do not rebel against the Lord, nor fear the people of the land, for they are our bread; their protection has departed from them, and the Lord is with us. Do not fear them."— Numbers 14:6-9

It's important to note that it was the Hebrew spies who talked themselves down. The giants never said a word. But wide is the gate that the majority takes, and the ten overruled the two. This should be a sober warning for us. Fearing man or obstacles will cause you to cast your opinion and vote yourself out of God's timing and your destiny.

You would think amnesia would have lifted from at least a few of the ten, but as Caleb and Joshua finished their speech the crowd gave a standing rebuttal.

And all the congregation said to stone them with stones...Numbers 14:10

For trying to talk the people out of fear and rebellion and into their destiny they almost got stoned. Too often we bite the hand that fends for us, and rebel against the One who delivered us. God was angry with His children and wanted to disinherit them. Fortunately, Moses negotiated a pardon with God for the people.

Rebellion carries severe consequences. For their refusal to enter into their place at God's designated timing, a forty-year sentence of wandering around in the wilderness was handed down. They talked of dust, now they would eat it. The gate into their promised land had a forty-year timer on it, and over 500,000 warring men will not live to see it open again. (See Numbers 1:45-46.)

Only two men of fighting age will survive the timer. Some of the wandering we may go through in life will be the result of poor decisions made by those we spy with. Their fear can shift us out of God's timing, if we are part of a united effort to go somewhere and get overruled. But His best still awaits those who remain faithful until the timer rings again.

Joshua became the new leader of Israel and the words of Caleb still echo in our ears today. He told his new commander and friend Joshua what we should tell our leaders after an extensive journey with them. Forty five years later, they were in their Promised Land and had displaced many of their enemies.

Joshua had already allotted lands to different tribes, and in Joshua 14:6 the tribe of Judah went to Joshua in Gilgal for their allotment. Caleb, whom was chosen from the tribe of Judah to spy out the land earlier, was with them. He and Joshua were the only two that had wholly followed the Lord and withstood the crowd that day.

Caleb addressed Joshua and reminded him that he was forty years old when they spied together and eighty-five now. He added:

"As yet I am as strong this day as on the day Moses sent me; just as my strength was then, so now is my strength for war, both for going out and for coming in."—Joshua 14:11

In forty-five vigorous years, Caleb had not lost any of his vitality or ambition. He still wanted what God promised him forty five years ago.

"Now therefore, give me this mountain of which the Lord spoke in that day..."—Joshua 14:12

Caleb outlived the 40-year timer and spent five years helping the nation conquer their enemies. Now he wanted the mountain God promised to him. Shouldn't we?

The inhabitants of that mountain just happened to be many of the giants that triggered so much fear in the ten spies that caused the revolt. He didn't care if the feared Anakims (giants) lived there. He was no more afraid of them at eighty-five than he was at forty! Caleb was confident that God who had been at his side for so many years was not about to depart now that it was his time.

Gates have timers! Joshua and Caleb entered the second opening of the gate to their promised land due to the stand they took at the first. Five more years of warfare seemed to only add fuel to Caleb's fire. The giants yet lived in the mountain but it didn't belong to them any longer. That mountain belonged to Caleb! He heard God promise it to him forty-five years ago.

And Joshua blessed him and gave Hebron (a high and strategic place) to Caleb the son of Jephuneh as an inheritance.—Joshua 14:13

It's never over until we fold our cards. Many of you reading this, as well as I, can relate to Caleb's life. We've spied and wondered with some and warred with others, but stayed faithful to God and made many deliveries along the way. Our destinies are worth persevering.

Now it's time to inherit that place God has promised us. It may have taken longer than we envisioned, but God has not left our side. How long we've waited is not a factor. If we are determined to have our mountain still, we must war and take it. The Greater One is in us.

The Bible says in Joshua 15:14; that Caleb drove out the giants from his Mountain. We will fight for what we are assured is ours.

Gates have timers! Be ready to walk in and war when God's timer sounds for you to enter into your destined place. He will go before you at that strategic time, and it will be your easiest time to take what He has promised you.

Be prepared and listen for the bell! It may not be a cake walk, but when you move with God, things will go well.

Chapter Eight

A Date with Destiny

Now the Philistines gathered their armies together to battle, and were gathered at Sochoh, which belongs to Judah; they encamped between Sochoh and Azekah, in Ephes Dammim. And Saul and the men of Israel were gathered together, and they encamped in the Valley of Elah, and drew up in battle array against The Philistines.—I Samuel 17:1-2

And a champion went out from the camp of the Philistines, named Goliath, (a giant) from Gath, whose height was six cubits and a span (over nine feet tall). —1 Samuel 17:4

And the Philistine said, "I defy the armies of Israel this day; give me a man that we might fight together," When Saul and all Israel heard these words of the Philistine, they were dismayed and greatly afraid.—1 Samuel 17:10-11

Jesse was miles away and knew none of this, but was nervously pacing the floor. "I should have heard from my boys by now," he thought. "Had the battle gone wrong? The army should be parading through town with spoils of war by today. They had been there for forty days! Had they lost track of time?"

Jesse made a quick decision, and sent for his youngest son David. One way or the other, Jesse knew that if the battle wasn't over, his sons and King Saul's army were in serious trouble. There was no time to lose.

He gave David an ephah of grain and ten loaves for his three older brothers and ten cheeses for their captains as well. He knew his brothers made fun of him, but he commanded his youngest to run to his brothers and see how they fared.

This sounded urgent, so David obeyed, rose early, and ran to the army camp. He never questioned his father's choice to send him, even though he had four older brothers at home. Jesse wasn't one for many words, and his brothers weren't fond of running errands. Everything worked out just great! He wanted to check things out at the battle front anyhow. Being a messenger boy that day caused things to go his way.

He hurried like he was told, and got there quickly. He left the supplies with the keeper and ran to greet his brothers at the battle front. As he talked with them, a strange scene began to unfold. In the distance, a giant of a soldier came up from the enemy ranks. He had a booming voice and was ranting and raving obscenities at Israel's army. Some of the soldiers said this had been going on forty days. Without knowing it, the giant lit a fire of righteous indignation in David.

And the Philistine drew near and presented himself forty days morning and evening.—1 Samuel 17:16

"Who was this guy?" David thought, "And why was he allowed to curse the armies of Israel and belittle their God? This brought shame on the Nation of Israel and their God. It should not be tolerated! Why was he given so much space?"

As the towering figure drew closer, the whole army ran to hide. Shocked by their actions and the fear on their faces, David asked, "Why are you running?"

"Have you seen Goliath, the giant?" the men asked. "He comes out every day to defy Israel. The King has offered a huge reward to anyone who kills him."

Their hiding and the mention of a reward turned David's head. He asked the soldiers nearby, "What kind of reward would a man get for killing the Philistine?" They replied, "King Saul has promised he will give him one of his daughters for a wife, and the man's entire family would be exempt from paying taxes."

Wow, being exempt from paying those hated new taxes that his father griped about would be great. When Israel chose to have a King like all the other nations, taxes were included. Palaces don't come cheap.

To rid David's large clan from paying taxes would be a blessing from Almighty God. And being given one of the King's daughters for a wife, you would need to be tax free. She wouldn't likely be low-maintenance. "Why hadn't somebody taken the King up on his generous offer?" David wondered.

Others Will Try to Talk You Out of Your Destiny

David asked another group of men about the reward and they gave the same answer. But when his oldest brother Eliab heard his little brother talking to the soldiers and asking questions about the reward, he became angry.

> *Now Eliab his oldest brother heard when he spoke to the men; and Eliab's anger was aroused against David, and he said, "Why did you come down here? And with whom have you left those few sheep in the wilderness? I know your pride and the insolence of your heart, for you have come down to see the battle." And David said, "What have I done now? Is there not a cause?"—1 Samuel 17:28-29*

Eliab's pride was fatally injured by kid brother's interest in taking out the giant. David seems to hurl back a question that even insults him more. In essence he asked, "Doesn't it seem to you I'm here for a reason?" Then he moved away from Eliab and on to another group of soldiers.

It would benefit us to remember that when Jesse ordered David to go check on his brothers, he arose early and left. Resentment failed to hold him back, and Eliab would soon be glad of it.

However, David knew he couldn't return to his father with this kind of news. The voice of Goliath had paralyzed his sons, the soldiers, and King Saul with fear. He decided to stay a while against his brother's wishes and get a closer look at this giant. Plus, the word *reward* was screaming like an eagle in his mind.

He would keep his distance from the brothers, dig a little deeper, and listen to God for his directions. After all, Eliab was hiding in a hole, too.

Destiny Has a Familiar Sound

It seemed destiny was knocking, but David had to be sure. He was beginning to understand why Jesse chose him for this errand. He had told his father about the lions and the bears he had killed while protecting his sheep. Jesse had looked surprised but had believed the wild stories his youngest had told him.

But how did his father have the intuition that the army was in trouble? He had just heard another soldier say they had been in this state for forty days.

Did the God who stopped the rain after forty days and nights tell my father that He was ready to stop this pelting of insults and fear?

Did the one who called Moses from the back side of the desert after forty years call my father Jesse to fetch me from the field?

The knock of destiny became louder and louder, but there was much on the line to consider. Though David was young, he was full of wisdom and knew to behave wisely. He was well aware of how things might appear if God chose him to deliver Israel from the disgusting plight they had dug themselves into. Many a man had lost his head due to the resentment of Kings. He must have God's signal to move. But the knocking had become a pounding in his belly that he had to reckon with.

> IT SEEMED DESTINY WAS KNOCKING, BUT DAVID HAD TO BE SURE.

Could it be the same God that looked on Leah's affliction and delivered her had looked on Israel's affliction and was ready to deliver him?

Did Israel's God show Jesse how King Saul and his army had lost sight of their covenant rights and vision? How they were wandering around hiding in holes.

And finally, was this just by chance, or could it be for real? God chose Moses' successor Joshua to lead the people across the Jordan. Did God call him here to lead His army out of this wilderness and across the valley?

"Lord, is this what You have been preparing me for?"

David reasoned all these things in his heart. Then he understood why his father had become so anxious. He knew time had run out. Something was fixing to break! He knew God needed someone to crack it open. David was becoming ever surer that someone was him. The soldiers told him of the forty days, but failed to grasp what time it was. Little did they know God was speaking through them?

The Number 40 is linked to Purging, Cleansing, and Spiritual Preparation through Testing

Forty days of insulting remarks from Goliath had stripped King Saul and his military men of their pride. But was this a hint of something deeper to come? David could still feel the warm oil the Prophet Samuel had anointed him with. It somehow had penetrated deep below skin level. For a few seconds, he was mesmerized about how it had flowed down over his face. Some had dripped off his chin while the rest found its way over his chest. It seemed like only yesterday. Nothing much had changed since then. Would that all change today?

If God delivers a victory to Israel, Saul and his army will have no reason to boast. After forty days of wondering what to do, they would realize only God has the answer. It is not by their might. Who of them could be prideful again the way they coward in fear here?

God had allowed Goliath to broadcast his daily views for forty days. He was akin to some of the broadcasters in the media mountain of today. He had the children of God paralyzed with fear and hiding from their call to be warriors. He had even blown their leaders out of their zone with his ruthless tone.

The name Goliath means to exile with splendor, deprive, to publish it, to remove, strip away, and run down. He lived up to his name back then and still does today. He uses his voice to try to convince the children of God they are a beaten lot and should surrender. It seems his voice has an echo and we all hear it at some time or another.

He had pelted his listeners with his bad morning show for forty days. He repeated the same message each evening just to make sure they didn't sleep well. Their world was crumbling fast and his audience was reeling like drunkards. It looked like they'd be his servants soon, not just listeners. No one had the courage to challenge him or his views. They were captives of fear. It was a tormenting sight to see.

> POSITIONS COME AND GO WITH THE
> WIND, AND ANOTHER UNKNOWN VOICE
> HAS JUST BLOWN IN.

It's amazing how history repeats itself. There's nothing new under the sun. On what looks like the 41st morning show of his illustrious career, Goliath still hasn't come up with anything new. Why should he? The re-runs were working well—Saul and army were still hiding.

However, nothing down here lasts forever. Positions come and go with the wind, and another unknown voice has just blown in. He was only a little over half the height of Goliath's nine foot stature but has the heart of a lion. He ruffles a few of his brother's feathers with his attitude as he passed through the crowd, but it was only a hint of things to come.

It's a pity no one in Saul's army realized what time it was. Not even the King himself understood. And of course Goliath was king of his mountain, and it was clear he was blinded with arrogance. It is absolutely amazing how two well outfitted armies had no one in charge of the time clock. History repeats itself.

Goliath was like many, and thought time was on his side. Israel was paralyzed. He was the hero of the hour and had gotten accustomed to the guys buying him drinks. He was after what you call field promotion.

He's nine-feet tall and covered in bronze from head-to-toe. They call him a champion wherever he goes. He carries a spear the weight of a deer. And there's a sword in his belt that cause opponents to melt.

But I have a question about this guy—if he was so mighty and ferocious, why hadn't he attacked already? Why run your mouth forty days? Just do it and be done with it! I for one, get tired of hearing what people are going to do. Show me what you've got or move out of the way. Was he into war or propaganda?

I believe Goliath was like many of our enemies today. He wore the right clothes and used the right vocabulary to attract attention and instill fear, but his pride had blinded him. He over-extended himself! He had his weaknesses. He was obnoxious, and knew very little about backyard business. He was on Israel's turf now and nobody had to go by his rules. Slingshots were legal in Socho.

It seems he was also unaware of how Israel's God fought for them. Evidently he had not been briefed about what happened to

Egypt, Jericho, and the others. Maybe his generals withheld that bit of info from him on purpose.

AFTER 40 RE-RUNS, GOD HAS HEARD ENOUGH!

All we know for sure at this point is that he has one whale of a mouth. I believe he is better at bluffing than fighting, like somebody else we know. Nonetheless, the shadow of the sun-dial was moving, and like Pharaoh, he has had ample time to correct his ways. After 40 re-runs, God has heard enough! One more night with the frogs was a party compared to what's in store for Mr. G. If he was as wise as he was loud, he would close his show down and leave the mountain. But no, he's on a roll.

The problem with giants is that they have giant mouths. But it had come the time to hush or be hushed. God could have led Jesse to rush David off because the time of pride purging was up, and the table was set for his youngest. Or, Jesse could have known the chips were fixing to fall one way or the other. The Bible doesn't clearly say, but it strongly implies this was a set-up either way.

We only know that all of a sudden, Jesse had an intuition, made a quick call, and sent his youngest off in a hurry. We know the 41st day is about to break, and a teenage boy heads to the battle. He is seemingly of no importance to anyone. He is just on an errand, taking provisions to brothers that ridicule him.

The errand boy carried significantly more than just food to the battle though. He brought vision along with the provisions.

The first was more essential than the latter. He saw what the army failed to see.

Where there is no vision, the people perish (wander aimlessly): but he that keepeth the law, happy is he.— Proverbs 29:18 [KJV]

When there is no vision to see what God is up to, or anticipate what His desires are, people are clueless of how to act. This was the state David found King Saul and his army. They had been wondering around aimlessly for forty long tormenting days.

The Philistine giant that looked so overwhelming to Saul's Army, didn't look so big to David. He had killed lions and bears bigger than him, and both could roar louder. David was all too familiar with this scene. He was in his element.

Timing Isn't Everything—It's an Open Door

To everything there is a season, a time for every purpose under heaven...—Ecclesiastes 3:1

The shepherd boy surveyed the army's reaction to the invitation of Goliath for a man to come and fight. Not a soldier moved a muscle, and the Captains cringed. The voice of fear held them speechless and immobile.

It looked like instant death to anyone who would dare face the giant. There was a unanimous vote in King Saul's army to continue paying taxes, and no one wanted his daughter as wife. What a plight.

> FORTY ONE MORNINGS WITHOUT A SINGLE VOLUNTEER WAS THE SIGNAL HE WAS WAITING FOR!

But on the other hand, David saw it as a God-ordained opportunity for him to enter the fray. Forty one mornings without a single volunteer was the signal he was waiting for! The fullness of time had come.

God is no respecter of persons. He will choose the weak to confound the wise. A teenage shepherd boy will work just fine. Humility will place you in the right place at the right time if you are ready for promotion and willing to move at God's beckoning.

When we have a gift, call, or ability in a certain area we should see opportunities there that others may not. Our vision should be keener where our gifting is. We should realize we are gifted in these areas.

David was young, but he was a man of war. He had the vision to see the battle as God saw it. The just shall live by faith. The battle scene changes drastically when you look through the truth of God's word. What appeared to be obvious defeat was victory concealed with the opposite appearance. Our ears and eyes must be in stride if we're to act and change the tide.

The pounding of war drums inside the shepherd boy confirmed his suspicions. He was the only one there covenant-minded and fully aware of what day and time it was. Whether Jesse knew it or not, his notions were correct. The media mountain had to have a new voice today. David was now assured this was *his date with destiny*, and he was more than willing to deliver.

The noise of a giant is no measure of his strength, and Goliath's arrogance has only bolstered David's decision to step forward. This agent of deception has deceived himself and Saul's army into believing he was something special. The only one present he hadn't convinced was the errand boy.

A man's gift makes room for him, And brings him before great men.—Proverbs 18:16

Word circulated to King Saul that a young boy wanted to take on the giant. The King called him in and half-heartily tried to talk him out of it. "You're nothing but a kid!" he exclaimed. However, the kid was his only volunteer. He slowly realized the only hope of Israel escaping defeat and bondage to the Philistines probably stood in front of him. What a mess they were in.

He had to humbly agree with the shepherd boy and gave him his own armor to fight the giant. David could not even walk in it. He had to remove it.

David assured the King there was no reason to fear. The same God that delivered him from the paw of the lion and bear would also deliver him from this Philistine. The King heard courage speak and said, "Go, and God be with you."

He walked out of Saul's tent and into history. He picked up his staff and slingshot along the way and left the crowd behind. The army watched in stupor as the boy got even smaller as he drew nearer to the giant. He paused at a brook, picked up five smooth stones, and kept walking, sizing up Goliath step-by-step.

> **Forty days had come and gone. Israel had to move on!**

He saw the giant's helmet was unable to cover such a head. It had left him vulnerable. A portion of his forehead was clearly visible up close. He could even see wrinkles in it when he cussed. David hoped Mr. G. would lean over a bit, and with God's help he planned to add a couple of more wrinkles to it.

Goliath began to curse David angrily, but his words failed to shake the boy's confidence. He cursed even louder as the shepherd boy approached closer. He was infuriated and insulted that King Saul would send such a small boy to fight one so fierce.

"How dare you send a boy with sticks to me!"

He swore by his gods that he would feed David to the birds of the air and beast of the fields. That was his last broadcast. He was about to go off the air.

The boy with the new voice wasted no time. He was ready to speak and broke the stalemated atmosphere like a bolt of lightning on a dark cloudy day. His words lit up the sky like the

Fourth of July. His first broadcast was full of faith, clear, and powerful. His righteous indignation roared like a lion, and set the stage for an upset. Forty days had come and gone. Israel had to move on!

Then David said to the Philistine, "You come to me with a sword, with a spear, and with a javelin. But I come to you in the name of the Lord of hosts, the God of the armies of Israel, whom you have defied. This day the Lord will deliver you into my hand, and I will strike you and take your head from you. And this day I will give the carcasses of the camp of the Philistines to the birds of the air and the wild beast of the earth, that all the earth may know that there is a God in Israel." —1 Samuel 17:45-46

David knew his God could do exceedingly abundantly above all that he could ask for or think, so he took advantage of it. He had his sights set on more than just Goliath—he was only one of many.

To Goliath's surprise, the boy was running toward him now with a staff in one hand and his slingshot in the other. All of his threats hadn't phased the boy one bit. David had already slipped the first smooth stone into his sling and had it circling above his head building momentum. The closer they got, the bigger David's target became. He didn't let the giant's size intimidate him anymore than the lion or bear.

Goliath was so tall he had to look down at the shepherd boy. This was what David was waiting for. By now the stone in his sling had reached the velocity needed to down a giant.

David aimed his first rock well and turned lose one string of his sling. The stone seemed to have a mind of its own. A shocked expression came over Mr. G. as he rubbed his forehead in disbelief as he fell forward to the ground. His broadcasting days were over.

Now I can almost hear Eliab yelling, "That's my little brother, isn't he something?" Another brother yells, "Let's get after those fleeing Philistines." One spontaneous reaction from David turned the tables on the enemy. Israel then routed them.

With a slingshot and a boy, God saved a nation that day from going into bondage. We must be willing to use what He equips us with. David never asked to borrow another man's weapon. He used the sling in his hand with confidence that God had gifted him with.

David was sent to the battle to deliver a message and a stone that would free an army. That sequence of events had far-reaching effects. They set in order the transition for him to become the most celebrated King of all Israel's history.

He delivered only a part of his destiny that day, but how the fireworks went off in Israel.

Many of you reading this page are just like David was that day. You are moving with your destiny, but at times you are still running errands. Stay in shape.

David thought he'd been given another insignificant assignment, but was happy to rise up early and go. He was oblivious to the needs or opportunities that lay waiting, and we all are to some degree.

He had the goods which the army in bondage needed so desperately. He delivered them and changed his and many other lives forever. Fireworks continue to go off each time this thriller is told all over the world.

You may be asking when something of this nature will happen to you. I can only answer what has been a trend in my life and others. When God gets us prepared, when His time is right, and when we least expect it, opportunities for deliveries and promotion seem to come.

Be prepared and willing to wait. God has your name on His calendar. Destinies have dates.

Chapter Nine

Serving Leads to Romance and More

Her decision was like iron. It was unyielding. Ruth had settled the question long before it would ever be asked. She wasn't about to let her aging mother-in-law make the long trek back to her country alone. She had witnessed a robust Naomi be drained of life by one heartache after another. Only a shell was left of the talkative fun-loving person she used to be. Naomi was aging and had dropped hints of wanting to return to Israel while she was still able. Who could blame her? Moab had been merciless.

Ruth knew firsthand the grief Naomi had endured, but was well aware she still reverenced her God. Her misfortunes had not separated her from her faith. Why the Lord God of Israel had allowed life to deprive Naomi so was unclear.

In the past she had often shared with her daughters-in-law about the greatness of her Lord. Ruth terribly missed those captivating times. There was something in her that longed to know more about her mother-in-law's miracle working God. She had never heard of any god that could part a sea to deliver a nation. She wanted to hear more, and plus deserting one which had become closer than a mother to her was against everything Naomi stood for. She was compelled to tear herself from her own to be with Naomi when the time came.

Naomi's husband Elimelech had made the decision to uproot his family from Bethlehem, Judah in Israel, during a time of famine. They had come to the land of the Moabites about ten years ago seeking relief. Unfortunately, Elimelech died after they settled in Moab. This left Naomi with only her two sons living in a foreign land. That was only the beginning of her sorrows, more were to come.

The names of her two sons were Mahlon and Chilion. Ruth had met and married Mahlon. Another Moabite girl named Orpah had married Chilion. It looked as if life had decided to shine once more on Naomi, but it was short-lived.

As time went on, Ruth's husband Mahlon and Orpah's husband Chilion both died. Grief had become the Matriarch's common companion and death her enemy. Yes, of course, it had been very painful for the girls, but they were young enough to marry again and have families. Naomi was too old for either.

She suffered the loss of her husband and both sons. And worse yet, neither Mahlon nor Chilion had produced an heir. That was the curse of all curses. Without a husband, sons or grandson, she was without an heir and a future.

After her sons died, both girls stayed with Naomi. There was a knitting of souls through the deaths of their men. It seemed the thread of sorrow had sown them together in their time of need.

Naomi never complained much about her husband's choice to move the family to Moab. Maybe it was for fear of hurting the girls' feelings, but she had only seen hardship and death since they came. Through it all, she still had the will to keep going, but she did think the hand of her God was against her for some reason. Or could it be the land of Moab viewed her family as intruders and aimed to snuff them out? She longed to move home.

The Opportunity Comes

After ten long years, Naomi finally received good news. The famine had lifted in Israel. She saw her time was up in Moab and quickly determined to move back to Judah. Ruth was previously prepared, but Orpah's decision to leave Moab too was a bit of surprise. However, both women packed up their belongings and headed out of town with Naomi.

Therefore she went out from the place where she was, and her two daughters-in-law with her; and they went on the way to return to the land of Judah.—Ruth 1:7

As they went on their way, Naomi's nobility was called into question. It was still there. Pierced by daggers of reality, she shouldered the truth. She had left her country in a time of famine, but at that time she had a husband and sons. At that time she had something to offer a daughter-in-law. Death had changed all of that. She had nothing to offer anyone now but poverty and hard times. She loved her widowed daughters-in-law. They had been good wives to her sons and gracious to her as well. They had even looked upon and been closer to Naomi than their own mothers. She had to consider their best interest.

Was it fair to let them attach themselves to a woman too old for a husband and no means of support? They had willingly volunteered to go and she needed them more than the donkey under her, but how could she justify ruining their futures? How could she live with herself and could she make it alone?

However, the voice of her conscience, became stronger than her needs. It would not be ignored any longer. She pulled up on her animal's reigns to stop quickly before she changed her mind.

And Naomi said to her two daughters-in-law, "Go, return each to her mother's house. The Lord deal kindly with you, as you have dealt with the dead and with me."—Ruth 1:8

Without asking either, Naomi called on the Lord to help them find rest in the houses of new husbands and kissed them farewell. They lifted up their voices and openly wept. Both pleaded with her that it was their choice to return to Israel with her. Their insisting fell on deaf ears.

But Naomi said, "Turn back, my daughters; why will you go with me? Are there still sons in my womb, that they may be your husbands? Turn back, my daughters, go—for I am too old to have a husband..."— **Ruth 1:11-12**

Naomi had lost her husband, sons and everything else except life itself. She was in a place of despair but had to tear herself from her faithful daughters, as she called them. She couldn't bear the guilt of the difficult impoverished life they would live with her.

Age and death had worked hand-in-hand against her the last ten years. Those closest to her had not fared well. Her faithful daughters could be next to die if they didn't turn back. Both lifted up their voices and wept loudly once more. How silently life had knitted these three together, and now was tearing them apart.

Orpah finally calmed down and reality formed a picture in her mind. She kissed her mother-in-law good-bye and turned back. She returned to her family and the gods of the Moabites. She was never heard of again.

But Ruth did the unexpected. *She clung to Naomi.* This was the day she had prepared for long ago. She had it fixed in her mind to cling to more than just Naomi. She was deserting the gods of the Moabites to cling to the God of the Israelites.

> SHE SOMEHOW KNEW THAT IN SERVING HER MOTHER-IN-LAW, DESTINY WAS HAVING ITS WAY WITH HER.

This was an affirmation of her faith in Israel's God, Yahweh. Ruth adopted herself into every fabric of Naomi's life. She somehow knew that in serving her mother-in-law, destiny was having its way with her. So be it, she reasoned. What the outcome would be wasn't a factor. She was determined, took her stand and followed in the footsteps of Abraham without knowing it. She made the strongest case one could make.

But Ruth said: "Entreat me not to leave you, Or to turn back from following after you; For wherever you go, I will go; And wherever you lodge, I will lodge; Your people shall be my people, And your God, my God. Where you die, I will die, And there will I be buried. The Lord do so to me, and more also, If anything but death parts you and me." —Ruth 1:16-17

Sandwiched in the middle of her delivery was the statement, "Your God shall be my God." Mahlon had also told her about Yahweh. She declared in the middle of the road that day where she would travel forever.

She had seen Naomi targeted like no other. Her losses had been heavy. Her ten years were up. Now she just wanted to go back to her homeland. Ruth believed leaving her family and gods behind was the right thing for her to do. She grafted herself into the vine of service. Wherever that vine swung her was fine.

> ## SHE GRAFTED HERSELF INTO
> ## THE VINE OF SERVICE.

Stunned for a moment by Ruth's declaration of faith, Naomi is taken back. She knew Ruth well. She was aware her mind was made up and there was no changing it. She wondered when Ruth decided this.

Naomi slowly loosened the reins on her donkey to prod forward. She had to look away from her daughter to hide the tears of appreciation. The trip to Bethlehem was dusty and silent. Their thoughts provided most of the communication. What kind of reception could they expect? A poor grief stricken widow was coming home with nothing except her widowed Moabite daughter-in-law. But the unexpected happened.

When they reached Bethlehem the whole city was excited to see them. The women said, "It this Naomi?" But she said to them, "Don't call me Naomi (which means pleasant and favored); call me Mara (bitter)." She went on to say, "I went out full, and the Lord has brought me home again empty." Had she forgotten about Ruth?

However Naomi felt, they couldn't have arrived in Bethlehem at a better time. The famine was over, and it was the beginning of the barley harvest. It was perfect timing for two women without any means of support. What a coincidence.

The Lord had instructed the Israelites through Moses not to completely harvest their fields. They were to leave some so the poor and strangers could gather it for their survival. Also, the poor could be allowed to glean (pick up what the reapers dropped) as they harvested the fields. A stranger might be given this opportunity also, but had a slimmer chance. By this provision in the Law of Moses, the poor could work and survive without being humiliated to the point of begging.

Naomi was still under the grip of depression, and Ruth realized it was time for her to step up. She had heard of the opportunity for the poor to glean, and realized they were perfect candidates. If they were to survive she must find a field to glean in and fast.

There was a relative of Naomi's husband, a man of great wealth, of the family of Elimelech. His name was Boaz. So Ruth the Moabitess said to Naomi, "Please let me go to the field, and glean heads of grain after him in whose sight I may find favor." And she said to her, "Go my daughter."—Ruth 2:1-2

Ruth was not asking for a handout. Gleaning was back-breaking work from sun up till sun down. You picked up the grain or heads of grain from the ground that the reapers dropped. She got up early the next morning and gleaned in the field after the reapers. Here again is another coincidence. The Bible says (in vs.3) "She happened to come to the part of the field belonging to Boaz." Imagine that.

And to top it all off, take a look at this. Boaz came from Bethlehem that day to his field at the perfect time. He somehow stood in the precise locality to notice an unfamiliar young woman (difficult the way they dressed back then) along with the other young women gleaning in his field.

These are the kind of everyday miracles that can happen when you serve others loyally. You are noticed and interest in you is aroused. Then you are asked about.

Then Boaz said to his servant who was in charge of the reapers, "Whose young woman is this?"—Ruth 2:5

Boaz wants to know who this diligent young woman is that is not too proud to work and pick up what the reapers drop. His servant answers (vv6-7), "It is the young Moabite woman who came back with Naomi from the country of Moab. And she said, "Please let me glean and gather after the reapers among the sheaves." So she came and has continued from morning until now, though she rested a little in the house."

Ruth (which means beautiful) didn't ask for a handout from anyone. She came to Bethlehem with a servant's mentality. Gleaning wasn't for the weak-hearted because there were others elbowing for what fell from the reapers hands too.

Ruth's reputation had preceded her. Boaz had heard only good things about this Moabite woman. It was no small secret how she left her home country to look after and serve the aged Naomi. She had actually become the talk of the town. He had been curious to meet this gem of a person and here she was in his field. He was a man of great wealth and didn't get there by shunning others. He wants to reward her for serving Naomi. With dignity Boaz approaches Ruth with honor and favor.

Then Boaz said to Ruth, "You will listen, my daughter, will you not? Do not go to glean in another field, nor go from here, but stay close by my young women. Let your eyes be on the field which they reap, and go after them. Have I not commanded the young men not to touch you? And when you are thirsty, go to the vessels and drink from what the young men have drawn."—Ruth 2:8-9

An Updraft of Favor

Ruth's life just took an updraft of favor. She literally felt the wind lift her. She was swirling in the protection and provision of Boaz now. He told her not to leave his field, but to stay with his young servant woman. He assured her that the young men wouldn't bother her either, and you can tell by these statements that Boaz was an older man. He also added that she could drink from the vessels the young men had drawn. He even thought of her thirst.

> IF YOU WANT TO KNOW HOW TO STEP INTO
> DESTINY, PATTERN YOUR STEPS LIKE RUTH'S.

If the same happened to us today, how many would say, "Well it's about time Mr. Favor came my way, I've been waiting long enough." That's the point our flesh would like to make anyway. But look at Beautiful's response to favor.

So she fell on her face, bowed down to the ground, and said to him. "Why have I found favor in your eyes, that you should take notice of me, since I am a foreigner?"—Ruth 2:10

If you want to know how to step into destiny, pattern your steps like Ruth's. She faithfully served the people God connected her to with a good attitude. She wasn't afraid of work, and was willing to take a different position to help herself and family. Ruth was more concerned with contributing than consuming. If this is your routine, you are already flowing with destiny and making deliveries. Hey, but it gets better. God is into progress and promotions! Here is Boaz's answer to Ruth.

And Boaz answered and said to her, "It has been fully re-
ported to me, all that you have done for your mother-in-law
since the death of her husband, and how you have left your
father and your mother and the land of your birth, and have
come to a people whom you did not know before. —Ruth 2:11

When you are willing to walk with God's plans at the expense of your own, it will be fully reported. The right people
will hear about it. You may never have heard of them, but they
will see you in their field of vision at the right time. Provision,
protection, and drink (anointing and revelation) can be given to
you at any routine moment in time.

Many are concerned about catching a blessing here or a word
there, but I have to ponder. How many of us by not being in the
right place at the right time with the right attitude have missed
out on our updrafts of favor?

Ruth left her land to fall in line with God's plan. She didn't
even know if she'd live to see Bethlehem. Travel was dangerous
in those days, especially for single women. Naomi had warned
her of poverty not prosperity, but she clung to her anyway.

Boaz then prayed for the Lord to repay Ruth for her remarkable loyalty and work, and a full reward be given her by the
Lord God of Israel, under whose wings he said she had come
for refuge.

We know he articulated the truth for she replied, "Let me
find favor in your sight my Lord; for you have comforted me
and spoken kindly to your maidservant, though I'm not like one

of your maidservants." Ruth now calls herself one of Boaz's maidservants. She no longer views herself as a foreigner.

Another Updraft of Favor

Now Boaz said to her at mealtime, "Come here, and eat of the bread, and dip your piece of bread in the vinegar." So she sat beside the reapers, and he passed parched grain to her; and she ate and was satisfied, and kept some back.—Ruth 2:14

Ruth was pulled up higher yet as Boaz invited her to the noon meal. He realized her and Naomi's plight and wanted to help any way he could without embarrassing her. She was now eating with the reapers and Boaz himself was passing the parched grain to her.

The Unusual Happens

When Ruth rose up to glean, Boaz did the unusual. He commanded his young men in the next verses, "Let her glean even among the sheaves, and do not reproach her. Also let grain (heads) from the bundles fall purposely for her; leave it that she may glean, and do not rebuke her."

Are things turning around for industrious Ruth or what? She's gone from an updraft of favor into a whirlwind of blessings. The Lord says in the Bible several times that if we'd humble ourselves He would lift us up. Ruth has humbled herself in an unusual way, and now the Lord is lifting her up at a most unusual pace. Where will it go from here?

Stricken With Beauty

I believe Boaz was stricken by the beauty of Ruth's character and more! I believe his soul was touched by her kindness (loyal love) to Naomi. I personally believe it was love at first sight— my opinion only. You can almost hear him thinking, "How I wish God would have brought this young woman under His wings into my field of life earlier. How wealthy I really would have been. If I could have noticed this treasure of a woman sooner what a wonderful life we could have had together. What a fine, happy, and God-loving family we could have been."

> I PERSONALLY BELIEVE IT
> WAS LOVE AT FIRST SIGHT.

He was not so bold as to let his thoughts become words. He allowed his emotions to speak only what he deemed proper. Ruth was a virtuous woman and he was a righteous man. God would have to take it further if He so willed. This is a lesson to all. When we are walking with destiny, the unusual happens.

Let us not forget that Ruth not only demonstrated loyal love toward Naomi, but also to the Lord God of Israel. When she left

Moab she literally turned away from their gods too. Naomi's God Yahweh is now her God. There are no foreigners in the Kingdom of God. All are accepted.

Before we go on, I would like to ask a question. Have you ever been born again? As God set the stage for Ruth to come out of Moab, He has set the stage for you too. He wants to provide protection for you through His Son Jesus Christ of whom Boaz is a type. He's calling you out of that foreign land to Bethlehem (House of Bread). He has an updraft waiting for you, and will provide, protect, and give you drink now and forever more in Heaven.

In John 3:1-2 a man named Nicodemus came to Jesus one night wanting to know more about Him, the Kingdom of God and how to enter in. Like most he was tip-toeing around the issue, but Jesus knew his need.

Jesus answered and said to him, "Most assuredly, I say to you, unless one is born again, he cannot see the kingdom of God."— John 3:3

This was all new to Nic. He was still confused, and asked Jesus how all this could take place?

Jesus answered, "Most assuredly, I say to you, unless one is born of water and the Spirit, he cannot enter the kingdom of God .That which is born of the flesh is

flesh, and that which is born of the Spirit is spirit."—
John 3:5-6

Nic still doesn't get it, but he's on the way. Jesus now gives him what he came for—the way to be born again.

"For God so loved the world that He gave His only begotten Son, that whoever believes in Him should not perish but have everlasting life. For God did not send His Son into the world to condemn the world, but that the world through Him might be saved."
—John 3:16-17

Nic was sure it would be rather complicated, but God proved him to be wrong. It was so simple, even a child could understand.

That if you confess with your mouth the Lord Jesus and believe in your heart that God has raised Him from the dead, you will be saved. For with the heart one believes unto righteousness (right standing with God), and with the mouth confession is made unto salvation.
—Romans 10:9-10

God has made it very clear how to be born again. When I took these steps I was shocked at what I'd been missing. Listen to the voice of God's Holy Spirit, let Him lead you through these simple steps and let your world change forever. It is much too great an offer to pass up.

> AS MUCH AS BOAZ WANTED TO PROVIDE
> AND PROTECT RUTH, THE HEART OF JESUS
> POUNDS HARDER FOR YOU.

As much as Boaz wanted to provide and protect Ruth, the heart of Jesus pounds harder for you. As much as Boaz wanted Ruth, he wouldn't force himself upon her. He had made the first move, and it was up to her now. She had to come to him. Jesus has demonstrated His love toward us via the cross. It's up to us to make the next move.

Ruth Keeps Gleaning

Many would have run home excited at this point heralding the news about how God came to their aid; not Ruth. She continued to glean in Boaz's field till evening and beat out (separate) the grain from the stalks she had gleaned that day. It was about an ephah of barley, which is about a half hamper.

When she got home and Naomi saw what she had gleaned, she could scarce believe it. When she ate what Ruth had kept back from lunch for her, hope reared up in her soul like a stallion ready to defend his herd.

After years of sorrow, fate changed in a day. Naomi's mountain of depression was whisked away by an ephah of barley grain. She felt weightless after many years of heaviness. She remembered what the favor of God looked and tasted like. She had just eaten some of it and was staring at more. Her anticipation after so many years got the best of her. She blurted out in a question form, "Blessed be the one who took notice of you?"

When Ruth informed her excited mother-in-law that it was Boaz's field she gleaned in, Naomi was beside herself with joy! When Ruth told her that Boaz invited her to join him and the reapers for lunch and even passed the parched grain to her, Naomi was humbled. She was fully aware now that when Ruth (beautiful) clung to Naomi (favor) it was none other than the grip of God Himself.

Then Naomi said to her daughter-in-law, "Blessed be he of the Lord, who has not forsaken His kindness to the living and the dead!" And Naomi said to her, "This man is a relation of ours, one of our close relatives (redeemers)."—Ruth 2:20

Naomi finally calmed down enough for Ruth to tell her the rest of her miraculous encounter. "He also said to me, 'You shall stay close by my young men until they have finished all my harvest."

BOAZ HAD SHOWN UNUSUAL ATTENTION AND GENEROSITY TOWARD RUTH.

With thoughts and ideas dancing together like lovers in Naomi's head, she replies in verse 22, "It is good, my daughter, that you go out with his young women, and that people do not meet or encounter you in another field." So Ruth continued to glean in Boaz's field of favor until the end of the barley harvest and dwelt with Naomi right on.

Favor had returned to Naomi's life because of Ruth and gears were turning in her head about her well-being now. Boaz had shown unusual attention and generosity toward Ruth. "Could there be affection hidden behind his acts of kindness also?" she wondered. He was an older man, but without a wife. And he was close enough of a relative to be their kinsmen redeemer if he chose. With Ruth unaware, Naomi was assembling a plan.

A kinsmen redeemer was accountable for protecting family members if they fell on hard times. Naomi had lost her husband and both sons and Ruth had lost her husband too, and both were without an heir. Here again both women were perfect candidates for redemption by a close relative. Life had drastically improved with Boaz's favor, but Naomi sensed pleasantness was to be given back too. Just how much more did God have in store?

How much a kinsmen redeemer could help in such cases related to how well off he was, and of course, what his immediate family could and would withstand. Some kinsmen could do little and others could do much. It was not a secret Boaz was a kind man of great wealth and without a wife. Common sense told Naomi he had the means and freedom to redeem as he so desired. Her mind was made up.

The barley harvest was over and the ideal time had come to ask Boaz to be their kinsmen redeemer. Naomi's faith had grown and she believed the Lord wanted to supply Ruth with even more. She informed Ruth of a bold kinsmen tradition and Beautiful agreed to do as she was directed.

> "TAKE YOUR MAIDSERVANT UNDER YOUR WING, FOR YOU ARE A CLOSE RELATIVE."

Boaz would be at the public threshing floor that night, and it would be quite a festive occasion. The men would be eating, drinking and celebrating the harvest. Naomi instructed Ruth to wash herself, anointed herself, put on her best garment and go down to the threshing floor. She was not to make herself known to Boaz until he had finished eating and drinking, and his heart had been made merry.

When Boaz had bid his fellow companions goodnight he went to lie down at the end of his heap of grain. Ruth then did as Naomi had commanded and went softly and uncovered his feet and lay down.

Now it happened at midnight that the man was startled, and turned himself; and there, a woman was lying at his feet. And he said, "Who are you?" So she answered, "I am Ruth, your maidservant. Take your maidservant

under your wing, for you are a close relative."—Ruth
3:8-9

When Ruth uncovered Boaz's feet and lay down there, she performed a bold dramatic act. But when she answered, "Take your maidservant under your wing, for you are a close relative" it was purely romantic. She had just proposed to Boaz. She literally asked him to protect and provide for her through marriage.

He knew exactly what she asked because he replied in (vs10) she was blessed of the Lord that she didn't go after younger men. His quick answer was proof he had deep affections for her.

"And now my daughter, do not fear I will do for you
all that you request, for all the people of my town know
that you are a virtuous woman."—Ruth 3:11

He had to tell Ruth there was a relative closer than him that could redeem her, and in the morning they would meet. They met the next morning and the other relative couldn't perform the duties of a close relative. Boaz proudly said he would take care of all the legalities and take Ruth the Moabite to be his wife. Boaz, like Christ was willing to identify with Ruth, who was a foreigner.

And all the people who were at the gate (of the city),
and the elders, said, "We are witnesses. The Lord make

*the woman who is coming to your house like Rachel
and Leah, the two who built the house of Israel; and
may you prosper in Ephrathah and be famous in Bethlehem.— Ruth 4:11*

All the leaders and elders at the gate of the city (where legal
matters were transacted) saw such traits in Ruth they elevated
her in prayer to be like Rachel and Leah, the two that bore the
twelve tribal leaders of Israel. What an honor!

Boaz and Ruth were married and she delivered him a son,
and they called him Obed. He was the father of Jesse and the
grandfather of King David, from which linage the King of kings
Jesus, was born.

Ruth served her way into another country, romance and
marriage. She was another servant that delivered her destiny and
took her place in history. A book of the Bible was named in her
honor, and destiny placed her in the genealogy of Jesus Christ
along with her husband Boaz and son Obed.

Serving may take you away from what's been the norm and
comfortable, but it may thrust you into your destiny. Look what
it did for Ruth!

No matter who you are or what country you live in, Jesus
is calling you out of foreigner status. He sees you as a Ruth
(beautiful) and longs for a romantic relationship with you.

There are no foreigners in the Kingdom of God, and like
Ruth, He has a position and place waiting for you.

Chapter Ten

Taxing Your Way into Destiny

Tax collectors may be frowned upon in our day, but were hated in Israel while they were under Roman oppression. Their Roman oppressors would appoint certain Jews with the capable skills to collect taxes. They made their living by receiving a commission of what they collected. They had to have the abilities needed to gather information and pen it for proof of their levies. They had to be good recorders. It was a must.

Many tax collectors went beyond what was fair and overcharged the people and pocketed the excess. Some became very rich at the expense of their fellow Jewish countrymen. You might say the Romans left the door wide open for more, and the greedy took advantage of the rich and poor. The Romans could care less.

It was just as difficult to hide prosperity back then as it is today. Tax collecting was a lucrative business and the properties and lifestyles of those in the profession proved it. The whole lot was despised by all Jews as charlatans for hire. The richer they were, the more detested they were. Nobody wanted anything to do with the swindling professionals except their own kind and whoever might profit from their company. The religious Pharisees pegged them just above those lost in sin and steered far from their company. However, Jesus took no offense toward them at all and even called one to be a disciple of His.

After these things He went out and saw a tax collector named Levi, (Matthew) sitting at the tax office. And He said to him, "Follow Me." So he left all, rose up, and followed Him.—Luke 5:27-28

Some would question why Jesus would lay his reputation on the line for such people. The Bible clearly answers.

For there is no respect of persons with God. —Romans 2:11 [KJV]

Hebrews 1:3 also says that Jesus is the express image God, so He doesn't chum up to one and shun another either.

I like Luke's account of what happened later at Matthew's house. It gives you a good picture and strong evidence of how brother Matthew had probably been tweaking the tax figures for some time to his advantage.

> *Then Levi gave Him (Jesus) a great feast in his own house. And there were a great number of tax collectors and others who sat down with them.—Luke 5:29*

Matthew had no small dwelling. A great number of his own kind and others were able to attend the feast he threw for Jesus at his own house. This man was wealthy. He had the means not only to throw a feast, but a great one. He had what you would call today a mansion, and the servants needed to entertain properly.

> THERE AREN'T MANY POSITIONS IN THE MARKET PLACE TODAY NOT TAXING IN SOME WAY OR ANOTHER.

This did not set well with the religious hierarchy of the day. Nor could they stomach Jesus associating with such without their sharp criticism. Look how they described the others who were there too.

> *And their scribes and the Pharisees complained against His disciples, saying, "Why do You (Jesus) eat and drink with tax collectors and sinners?"—Luke 5:30*

Jesus was never caught off guard with their slanderous questions and gave the perfect answer again. In (vs31) He said to them, "Those who are well have no need of a physician, but those who are sick."

You could go a hundred different directions here, but it seems to me many at the feast were sick with greed. The Healer was in Matthew's house and had already healed him of greed. He would never have departed with all that money on a feast if not. His goal was then to get his associates into the presence of Jesus and give them the same opportunity.

You may think you are in a taxing profession and may be. The business I was in for many years was taxing mentally and physically, and I was drained both ways almost every day. I asked often "Lord, with all I have gone through, are You sure I still have something to offer?" Be assured, we've all asked the same questions. There aren't many positions in the market place today not taxing in some way or another. But it doesn't matter what your occupation is, you have skills the Master wants you to deliver for Him.

Look how the bandit Matthew was called. Some may ask, "What did the Lord see in him that He could use and need?" Well, for starters, a tax collector had to know what was going on. He had to be one that was information-driven in order to levy the correct tax on all business transactions, plus a surcharge, of course. He also had to be a capable bookkeeper and record who owed what and how much they had paid to date. He had to be a person gifted for details. The Roman government didn't ask for it, they demanded it. You'd best not apply if you couldn't deliver.

Look how God used such an informative bookkeeper and detailed tax collector. Very little went unnoticed by the eyes of Matthew the disciple, and later, apostle. He penned to perfection the gospel that bears his name. He proved to the Jews (and the world) with detailed proof that Jesus was beyond a shadow of doubt, the Messiah. He referenced so much Old Testament prophecy which Jesus was the subject of and fulfilled that only the unwilling could doubt.

He informed with accuracy Jesus' genealogy from Abraham forward, and his gospel became the link that connected the Old Testament to the New.

The Lord gives us talents and abilities to make a living with and use for Him. Matthew had not one clue that his taxing abilities would tax him into his destiny and help him deliver the greatest story ever told.

Whatever your background or present state consists of, and whether you see it or not, there is something in it which will help deliver your destiny. You may be in the repair industry, raise children, or any number of occupations, but if Matthew worked his way into his destiny through his skills, so can you.

What may seem taxing now could be a foundation for your destiny.

Chapter Eleven

Fighting God's Will is a Fight to Lose

Have you ever opened an ordinary looking gift and received the surprise of your life with what was inside? Many of our destinies are wrapped in unfamiliar paper, and may not resemble anything we want to be associated with at first. What we often fail to see is that God likes to confound us with just how good He really is. Some like Matthew follow fast while others need more light.

God has our destinies planned, but like Saul of Tarsus many want it their way, and their pride has blinded them to any other. They believe they were taught the correct way, and would rather fight than switch. Like Saul, we can be stiff necked (unwilling to turn) and rebellious to the hilt. Some even go to extremes against any of a different mindset, and often take issue with those who are functioning where they should be. Saul was guilty of all.

Will God leave us on our road to disaster? No! He is Father first. He loves us too much to abandon us. He will keep working with us, but if we are determined to have it our way, there is a price to pay. He must knock us off our high horse ways and get us on the ground where we can listen. Saul of Tarsus gave the Lord no choice.

Then Saul, still breathing threats and murder against the disciples of the Lord, went to the high priest and asked letters from him to the synagogues of Damascus, so that if he found any who were of the Way, whether men or women, he might bring them bound to Jerusalem.—*Acts 9:1-2*

Saul was madly fighting against his destiny, and making very painful deliveries as well. He was convinced he was in the will of God, and therefore refused His urgings to change directions.

When we are fighting against our destinies, the Lord may have to use extreme measures to help us see things His way. The smarter we are the less painful it will be, and the less harm we will inflict on others. When Jesus had enough of Saul's rebellious behavior He gave him some of His light.

As he journeyed he came near Damascus, and suddenly a light shone around him from heaven. Then he fell to the ground, and heard a voice saying to him, "Saul, Saul, why are you persecuting Me?"—*Acts 9:3-4*

An army of people witnessed Saul's mighty fall that day when God's light (revelation) shone around him. When he fell off of his high horse he was blinded to his way forever. He had been more blatant than most, but was changed in a moment.

> ## ON THE GROUND HIS HEARING
> ## IMPROVED DRASTICALLY.

On the ground his hearing improved drastically. What he heard was unlike anything he ever imagined to hear. It sounded as if he had been fighting against the One he thought he had been fighting for. Saul had to know for sure.

And he said, "Who are You Lord?" Then the Lord said, "I am Jesus, whom you are persecuting. It is hard for you to kick against the goads."—Acts 9:5

Goads were sticks used to prod and urge livestock in the direction the herdsmen desired for them to take. Saul had fought hard against the Lord's urgings to stay his own course, and we all have at some point. But everything he was ever taught and fought for were drained out of him in an instant by Jesus' answer.

As any would react in such case before the Lord, he began to tremble as astonishment overwhelmed him. Saul had only one other question for Jesus, and in the next verse asked Him, "Lord, what do You want me to do?" That was all Jesus had been waiting to hear. He told him, "Arise and go into the city, and you will be told what you must do." He now had Saul's attention, and could share with him his intended destiny.

If you've been fighting against the will of the Lord for your life, you might as well fold your cards, Jesus holds the upper hand.

Jesus answered Saul's second question in the next few verses and his life was radically changed. He became a new man with a new mission.

One or both of those questions that Saul asked Jesus have more people tied up at their traffic jams than any other. When you have the answers to those two questions and engage, your life will never be the same. With some light on the subject of our destiny, the fighting will cease.

When the light turned green for Saul, he never looked back, and neither will you. A new person arose from the ground that day with a new mindset (wine skin). He was ready and willing to accept the new wine and direction for his future. It fit him perfectly and so will yours.

Some of the most prideful wayward people turn into some of the most on fire champions for God and deliver their destinies well.

The Lord turned a murderous Saul into the apostle Paul who wrote almost two thirds of the New Testament. He traveled and preached the world over, and met obstacles nearly every place he went. In the end he said that he'd fought the good fight of faith and finished his race. What a way to go out. That was his destiny.

When we unite with our destinies, it can be wilder and more fulfilling than we ever imagined. God doesn't live inside a box, and doesn't expect his children to live in one either.

Saul's determination to go his way could have alienated himself from God's plans for his life if the Lord hadn't intervened. Your destiny may not be what you think it is, but when you engage with it, you will have no regrets. It will be better.

Chapter Twelve

Your Destiny Should Fit You

What we are called to and gifted for are the very things we are prepped and designed for. They are tailor-made for us. No matter the success rate of other things, they are irregulars.

While traveling years ago, I stopped at an outlet mall to purchase a pair of jeans. Being surprised they had my size and in a rush, I hurriedly grabbed a pair and paid the cashier without trying them on. I felt good about getting what I wanted at a discounted price, and drove off. When I got home all my proud feelings vanished. One leg was a solid two inches longer than the other one. Why didn't I just try them on there to make sure they fit?

Of course, I had the receipt, so I could exchange them. But what good was that? The store was one-hundred-and-fifty miles back up the road. It's no use to lie; I got mad. When a garment is two inches off somewhere, it fits nowhere. I could cut them up or burn them, but I couldn't make them fit. They were irregulars.

> ## HIS GIFTS AND CALLINGS ARE THE ONLY ORIGINALS WE'LL EVER GET, AND THEY'RE THE ONLY ONES THAT WILL EVER FIT.

In God's outlets, this problem never occurs. He is the Master Tailor and aware of all of our measurements. There is no return policy needed, and He is not about to withdraw what He has gifted us with.

For the gifts and the callings of God are irrevocable (They can never be withdrawn).—Romans 11:29

The reason being, they are stitched beautifully and fit every curve in our complex make-up perfectly. It is up to us to identify, receive and proudly wear with confidence what God has given. If we aren't functioning in the correct apparel He has provided, it is no wonder we look so out of place at times. His gifts and callings are the only originals we'll ever get, and they're the only ones that will ever fit.

God is not into irregulars or misfits regardless of opinions. What kind of King wants an ambassador representing him in a suite that's two sizes too large or a dress two sizes too small? Not the King of kings. Our King wants us to be suitably dressed in clothes that properly fit. I never wear a suit to the beach. It's not a must to have the best either, but we should keep in mind Who we are representing.

With this in mind it is necessary to understand the natural order follows after the spiritual order. What we see came from what we didn't see. God created this earth and mankind with His word. He said in Genesis 1:3, "Let there be light, and there was light." The rest of chapter one describes in detail how God created the earth and everything in it. Every time He created something, He said something first.

What we see came from what God spoke into existence. He didn't bring part of Jupiter to form Earth. He created Earth and its décor and the animals, birds, reptiles and all the creeping things on earth by His spoken word. At the end of Genesis 1:25, the Bible says, "God saw that it was good." Then in verse 26, God said, "Let Us (Trinity) make man in Our image." Our DNA and makeup, came from the unseen spoken word of God. He formed our bodies from the dust of the ground, but we were lifeless until He breathed into us His breath of life.

I said all that to say this. If God doesn't want us looking like clowns in the natural world, He sure doesn't want us looking like clowns in the spiritual world. We tend to ignore we are spiritual beings which possess a soul (mind, will, and emotions) and live inside a natural body.

Furthermore, we have had human fathers who correct-ed us, and we paid them respect. Shall we not much more readily be in subjection to the Father of spirits and live?—Hebrews12:9

God is our spiritual Father and has given us natural and spiritual abilities because we operate in both worlds.

Now may the God of peace Himself sanctify you completely; and may your whole spirit, soul, and body be preserved blameless at the coming of our Lord Jesus Christ.—1 Thessalonians 5:23

For as we have many members in one body, but all the members do not have the same function.—Romans 12:4

Having then gifts differing according to the grace that is given us, let us use them...—Romans 12:6

We live in an Earth-suit for sure, but we must be aware the gifts and callings of God are streamlined by Him for us to function in both the natural and spiritual world. You simply need to be aware that God will not generally gift you with something out of your spiritual character. God is into order in both worlds. When He is properly represented, multitudes will want to be part of His family. That is why Jesus came.

God's gifts simply fit, and He wants you to recognize, develop, and deliver what He has gifted you with. Collision repair fit me perfectly. I loved to work on wrecked cars as a teenager, and realized I was gifted in that area. As time went on, it became my profession and God used and blessed me in it. Salvation brought light into what I did.

> ## ALL OF OUR GIFTS OVERLAP INTO BOTH WORLDS. WE DON'T LIVE IN BOXES.

After getting saved, I dove into the word of God and soon found out that I enjoyed teaching His word to others. Later on God called me to preach, and I began going to the county jail on Saturdays. There were a couple of large holding cells there along with several medium sized and small ones too. I could preach more out there in a day than I could in my home church in a year. Plus, it was a very diverse crowd and sometimes loud and challenging. You had to preach with conviction to be effective. It fit like a glove, and I learned early how to cut through barriers to connect with and help people.

Collision repair fit me for natural service and preaching for the spiritual. I served God and man with both gifts in both worlds. All of our gifts overlap into both worlds. We don't live in boxes.

I went on to build a thriving collision business, and served God all the while. Several years ago the Lord told me it was time to serve Him full-time, and at the right time, opened the door for me to leave.

It is imperative we stay tuned into God's word and prayer in order to hear Him concerning any decision of importance. I never had to wonder if I left at the right time. What appeared to be the worst time for me to leave my business was the perfect time. Romans 10:17 says, "So then faith comes by hearing, and hearing by the word of God." Your faith will be tested from time to time as we are constantly growing and that calls for alterations.

Faith to be refitted at odd times and against popular opinion is greatly enhanced by a healthy diet of God's word and prayer. He will also use dreams and visions to help direct you and keep you in time.

What God calls you to, He equips you for. I know people that are gifted in all types of professions. There are farmers, nurses, preachers, bankers and a host of others I can't see functioning in any other position. And there are those that can repair or construct anything. Thank God for the computer whizzes. God is the Master Tailor.

Many gifted singers, musicians, and white-and blue-collar professionals work with their natural abilities during the week and freely serve God with their spiritual gifts all the while. Then they serve God and man at our church gatherings. All of our gifts overlap to a degree.

Our choirs, sound booths, greeters, ushers, teachers and most of the helper positions in our churches are filled with people from various professions. They serve people with their natural and spiritual gifts wherever they are called. Experiment a little and see what fits you.

If you know you are called to something, but aren't equipped, God expects you to enroll in a school or college or take a position as you are led and get the training you need. Then He can help you excel in your calling. Faith to develop our gifts without some action will produce little fruit.

I mentioned earlier God wouldn't give you a gift out of your character, but there is a fine line here that many trip over. Do you know as much about your character and makeup as God does? I for one, do not. Let me explain.

As I stated in chapter two, I didn't understand with my mind what God was introducing to me so naturally I recoiled a bit. But then I made the decision to hear Him out and realized it was a perfect fit. You may balk at the first exposure or encounter of a new thing, but that doesn't mean it is out of your character. It simply means you aren't familiar with it yet. You're backing up only because your mind hasn't approved of it. That will pass if it is from God and you're willing to venture out.

> ## YOU CAN ONLY DELIVER TO OTHERS WHAT YOU HAVE.

For example, I have always loved ketchup and could never get enough of spaghetti sauce, but didn't like fresh tomatoes. It doesn't make sense does it? Then one day I looked at fresh cold tomato wedges on the salad bar and they spoke to me. "Try me," they said, "you don't know what you've been missing." I believed them, so I forked a few of the firmer looking ones and kept moving. My wife and I chose a table, sat down, and prayed. I was determined to try the tomato wedges first, before my taste buds were saturated with fried shrimp, fish, and cocktail sauce.

It was love at first bite, and still is. For some weird preconceived idea, I had rejected these now favorite friends of mine for thirty-five years. Change is good. I only want fresh cold tomatoes from the salad bar now. How fickle we humans can be.

I was an A student in English and Literature. It was a breeze to make A's without much study. It came natural. I've been a writer all my life, and it would shock most of my friends how many notebooks I have filled with management info, stories and messages. My business demanded creative writing often, so my abilities were enhanced further there. But I never broke the Algebra code. Guess what, I'm not an engineer.

I'm a hands-on guy; I went into the collision repair business where I had to write estimates and explanations all day every day. My hands were all over cars for years too. I also taught many others the collision business, and taught them well. You can only deliver to others what you have. I never taught Algebra to anybody.

I'm now using all the experience I gained through High School, Bible School, my vocation, ministry and life to move on and deliver more of my destiny. The time that many think they are losing in their professions is not a waste. Like Dr. Hagin often told us students, "If you're not learning what to do, you're learning what not to do." Both are essential.

Jesus was a Professional

The Bible teaches us to work with our hands, minds, and spirits to support ourselves, to give into the gospel and help the needy. Jesus had a vocation. That should tell us enough. There is no mention of Mary's husband Joseph being alive after Jesus was twelve years old. We can only assume he died somewhere after Jesus was twelve and before he was thirty or so. He is not mentioned when Jesus went into His ministry or noted in the family shortly after when Jesus went to His hometown preaching. They said of Jesus:

"Is this not the carpenter, the Son of Mary, and brother of James, Joses, Judas, and Simeon? And are not His sisters here with us?" So they were offended at Him.—Mark 6:3

Jesus was the eldest so the leadership and support of the family fell on His shoulders sometime during the time-frame just mentioned. I'm sure His brothers helped, but He was the male authority in the house after Joseph died.

If Jesus built furniture, I'm sure it was the best. Joseph trained Him in the vocation he was in, and you know he went far above the standard with what he knew about Jesus.

Your vocation, position, and those over you will help prepare you in some way for your destiny if you are in the right place. Jesus learned well how to work and care for others by experience. He proved it by going to the cross for us. He worked God's plan to save and support His family. The life of Christ is the greatest example any could follow to deliver their God given destiny. Jesus did it perfectly.

God is The Perfect Tailor and Life is a Fitting Room

Always keep in mind that God is the perfect Tailor and life is a fitting room. He wants to use us on and off the job. The better we follow Him, the better our destinies fit. Have you ever seen a tailor trying to size a person while they were shopping, exercising, or running all over town? No you haven't. They have fitting rooms. If you want to be sized correctly you must stand still for a while.

> ### IF YOU WANT TO BE SIZED CORRECTLY YOU MUST STAND STILL FOR A WHILE.

This may sting a bit, but it will help many of you. It is impossible for anyone (including God) to properly fit you for your destiny unless you allow them. If you are running from church to church, from job to job and from meeting to meeting you'll never get sized up. Visualize what a tailor's suit for you would look after you wore him out chasing you around for measurements— it wouldn't be pretty. And no, it wouldn't fit.

There is a reason for everything, and there is a season for everything. The waiting season gives nearly everyone on earth problems. However there is nothing that can or should take the place of spending intimate time alone with the Lord.

If you are called into the five-fold ministry like me and many others, waiting gives you a problem just like everybody else. We aren't anointed to wait. Many of us would be much better fitted to our gifts and calls if we'd spend more intimate time with the Lord. Not to ask Him for needs, but just be with Him. I will say it again, "Nothing replaces intimacy with our Lord."

It doesn't matter what vocation, ministry, or position you're in, Isaiah gave us all the best directions one could give for successful living.

But those who wait on the Lord shall renew their strength; They shall mount up with wings like eagles, They shall run and not be weary, They shall walk and not faint.—Isaiah 40:31

The reason so many are weary, frustrated, or have fainted is not due from missing some deep spiritual truth. They have missed or tried to shorten a season. It is simply due from not sitting still long enough before the Lord to get acquainted with Him and fitted for service. They left too early and are out of their season. Impatience drives many away from their fitting rooms and destinies.

Those that wait on the Lord renew their strength. That's what Caleb did! He remained with and waited on the Lord forty-five years. He was as strong at eighty-five as he was at forty. How did that happen? His strength was renewed as he waited on God. It took might to take Hebron, but Caleb mounted up with wings as eagles. His sharp eyes surveyed what God promised him and he took it.

I'm not implying it will take anybody forty-five years to get to their place. Caleb's case was special. However, it takes most of us longer than we anticipate, and we usually have to war when we get there.

> IT STILL AMAZES ME THAT THE CREATOR OF
> THE UNIVERSE FINDS OUR COMPANY AS
> SPECIAL AS WE FIND HIS, WHEN WE PULL
> AWAY AND SPEND TIME TOGETHER.

The Lord told me early on that writing was much like preaching. I had to be transparent to a degree in this calling too. He said, "Prideful preachers and writers are both failures." I must confess to you, it was just as, if not more difficult, for me to remain in the fitting room with the Lord as it may be with you. I've always been energetic, involved, and an outdoor person. I wanted to know what was beyond the next page and mountain and would push myself to see it. I continue to read quite a bit, but my 500 cc ATV does most of the climbing now. I still go, but by different methods. My wife maintains I still have OCD (obsessive-compulsive disorder), but I maintain I'm just me. We are both right to a point, I suppose.

However, she knows me better than anyone and will tell you I would rather be in the Lord's fitting room now than anywhere else. There is nothing that compares with being there. His provisions cause us to praise Him, but His secrets cause us to weep. It still amazes me that the Creator of the universe finds our company as special as we find His, when we pull away and spend time together.

I know waiting on the Lord in 2013 takes effort, and especially if you're raising a family, running a business or a number of other things. Much tugs on our time from many directions, but you can't afford not to spend time with the Lord. It will save you so much in the long run. Start by five minutes a day if your schedule is jammed. Stay committed and see for yourself how things will change. We lose a tremendous amount of time and money by not prioritizing what we have.

> MUCH OF OUR DESTINY WILL BE
> DELIVERED IN THE WORKPLACE AND
> IN OUR DAILY TRAVELS.

If I had spent more time in the fitting room earlier, issues which extracted much of my time and money could have been avoided. The stress levels are much lower in our lives when our mistake levels are lower. Spending time with the Master Tailor is the surest way for you to mount up with a destiny that fits and with less stress.

Multitudes in the Marketplace

I may burst your bubble, but there are far more people in the business world than in the church world. Every one of them has needs too. God wants to use you and me and our gifts to help those He leads our way. It is a known fact that only about three percent of Christians will be platform preachers. The other ninety-seven percent are supposed to preach from mobile pulpits of joy, love, and lifestyles. Our character and deeds in the marketplace should testify to all how great our Lord is. What we deliver there when the Lord opens a door will also help fit and prepare us for our destinies, too.

I have helped and been helped by many through intersecting with them at the marketplace. We all have the same basic needs, and the marketplace is where we purchase them. I love the surprises and set-ups of the Lord I walk into. It never ceases to amaze me how things unfold at times. All Christians are assistant pastors to a degree, and many people will be left unattended if you and I fail to step up in the business plazas of the world and be used.

Much of our destiny will be delivered in the workplace and in our daily travels. The harvest out there is truly great but it is the laborers that are few. At present the needs tremendously outnumber the deliveries. Chances are many prospects are headed your way. Most of Jesus' miracles took place outside the four walls of the church. It seems like He was making a point. If we fail to see to them outside, they will never come inside.

Destiny is not foolproof! It requires our attention. Be on guard and willing to embrace the new. Most of our reactions and deliveries in our daily travels are spontaneous. That may fit you better than you ever thought possible. You may never want to give it up!

Many are Searching While Functioning

For some reason, we are pronged to look across the fence at what seem to be greener pastures. Other callings, gifts, or abilities can look more appealing, but are they rational for us? I love good praise and worship music, but don't ask me to sing. I have problems with my new radio.

I know people that want to be in charge that dislike being accountable, and have precious little public relations skills. I'm at a loss of what you could put them in charge of. Many fail to realize the spotlight is a hot-light also. When I was in the collision business, I had employees who were positive they could manage better than I, but had a tough time getting to work on time. They didn't enjoy being under the heat either.

Some elders want to be the Pastor because of one hour a week of stage time. My question is, "What are your plans for the other 167 hours of the week?"

SPEND SOME TIME AND SEE WHAT FITS.

I ran into a guy a while back that was bouncing around in a meeting I attended. When he bounced my way we shook hands, and I asked him what his profession was. He smiled and said he was an apostle. If he was an apostle, I'm into Algebra.

Many are functioning in their calling, but still searching for it. How can you mature in what's yours if your eyes are on somebody else's. What has God put inside of you? What comes somewhat natural to you? That is where God will start you off. If you've never tried or experienced much, then avail yourself to what sounds right and try a few things on. Spend some time and see what fits. Take a gifts or helps evaluation, and see where your strong points are. Your destiny should fit you.

I have a friend that has one of the neatest ministries that I know of. He works a full-time job where he is a blessing. He and his wife are great servants in the church they attend. And his hobby is fixing up cars. He has helped many people by repairing their cars for what it cost him or less. He even buys problem cars and will tinker with them until they are reliable. Then he will sell them to people that need transportation without the bells and whistles. This man and his wife are both rays of sunshine to many. They have spotless reputations and deliver their destinies naturally.

> *If you want something that doesn't fit,*
> *watch out, you might get it.*

There are more accepted platform ministries in the church today than 25 years ago. In the area I grew up in if you were called to preach, you were a pastor or an evangelist. I evangelized and taught the word before going to Bible School, but planned to be a pastor afterwards. I had a family to support and couldn't work and travel too, and we were already living from Friday to Friday.

With this thought, I went into the pastor's class my last year. After graduation, things worked out in my area for a pastoral position, and I said yes. Did it fit? No. Will I ever try again? No again.

I highly respect pastors and have served and supported them far above most before and since. You may ask anyone I've served under. The reason that position doesn't fit me is because I am not called by God to it. The experience was good, but the position didn't fit my character or make up. Pastoring a collision business for 20 years suited me better. Any that have owned and operated a business or been in management understands thoroughly.

Try on Your Destiny by Serving Others

Serving others is another primary way to try on different apparel and enter into your destiny also. Many think serving others is a waste of their time, but nothing could be further from the truth. That is a lie of the devil.

"And if you have not been faithful in what is another man's, who will give you what is your own?"—Luke 16:12

Serving others is the easiest and by far the most economical way to see what does or doesn't fit. It's not your fitting room and the utility bill goes to another address. When your name is on the dotted line and then you find it doesn't fit, you are in deep yogurt.

Plus, you must grasp Jesus' point here whether it pricks you or not. If you can't be faithful in what belongs to a man or woman that you can see, who (surely not He whom you can't see) will (be foolish enough to trust you and) give you what is your own. Why? Because you have not spent time to serve and prepare.

You've got to read and listen between the lines on this one even further. Jesus also was alluding to the fact that He had something that belonged to the unfaithful one, but He couldn't give it to him. He lacked faithfulness and stability and would only bring reproach upon the Lord and hurt others in the process. I have seen many assume much, serve little, and go out unqualified and cause only damage.

> ## PROMOTION AND EQUIPPING COMES MANY TIMES BY SERVING OTHERS.

Jesus spoke those words, and how true they are. I owned and managed a profitable collision business and participated in the helps ministry all the while. I would do whatever I could to help my pastor keep things moving forward. Waiting on the Lord meant everything to me from toilet control to preaching Sunday mornings. I never knew what I'd be doing most times.

In the ministry of help, you assist others in their call and extend help to any that come their way. You will actually help some dial into what God has for them. Promotion and equipping comes many times by serving others. I have to look no further than the mirror and the Bible for proof.

I served under Pastor Larry Millender at Abundant Life Church in Tallahassee, FL for over eleven years while managing my own successful business. I supported him every way possible. I wanted him to flourish, and it didn't bother me to handle a trivial chore any more than an important one for him. And it didn't bother him when I would preach under the anointing or flow with the prophetic.

You only reap what you sow. When you serve others, you are sowing into their lives and ministries. Do you think those searching eyes of the Lord will overlook that? What you are reading is proof that He will not. I am not sure I would be writing books today if I had not served him as I did then. I still honor and take him to lunch when we can work it into our schedules.

If we go back a couple a couple verses, we see that Luke also made a point about how faithfulness in small things would lead to larger things.

"He who is faithful in what is least is faithful also in much..." Luke 16:10

Luke is the writer of Acts and the Gospel that bears his name. In Acts 6:5, he proved what Jesus said with the story of what happened to a man named Philip.

The early church was growing so rapidly they needed seven men of good report and full of the Holy Ghost and wisdom to manage the food program. Philip was chosen as one of the seven and he was serving the widows (not the apostles). He was faithful there, and evidently God began to distribute more than just food through his ministry.

Exactly two chapters later, in Acts 8:5, we find him in the city of Samaria preaching Christ. The Bible says that multitudes are heeding his words due to the miracles which he performed in their midst.

His ministry started out small. He served the widows first! When God had seen enough, He said, "Come on Philip, Samaria is waiting. They need Me and these miracles down there too." A mighty revival took place because one was faithful in a small thing first. God is into promotion.

> WHETHER THEY ARE IN OUR CLOSETS, MINDS, EXTENDED RELATIONS OR REGIONS, THERE ARE SOME THINGS THAT JUST NEED TO BE DISCARDED.

God will help fit and equip us for our destinies through serving others. As we try on different suites by helping in different positions, we are finding out what fits us. When I shop for clothes, I take the time and try them on before I buy them. Why try to wear what may not fit? We should be even more cautious about our destinies. What try to function in what God didn't fit us for?

Discard the Misfits

Most of us have purchased or bought into various things that we thought were right for us but upon using, wearing or connecting with, found out different. I doubt I'm the only one.

I've given away a ton of clothes that were too big for me. When I see eighty and ninety percent off nice garments I purchase some for others, but I now refuse to shelter, heat or air-condition anything that doesn't fit me.

There were some other things that didn't fit me either that I had to give up, walk away from or disconnect myself from too. If you are feeling irregular in an area, you may need to wake up and realize the same. Whether they are in our closets, minds, extended relations or regions, there are some things that just need to be discarded. Reading this scripture makes it easier for me.

Then He (Jesus) said: "A certain man had two sons. And the younger of them said to his father, Father give me the portion of goods that falls to me, So he divided to them his livelihood. And not many days after, the younger son gathered all together, journeyed to a far country, and there wasted his possessions with prodigal living."—Luke 15:11-13

The young son was determined to get his stuff and go his way, and his father decided to let him. He was aware his youngest was making a poor choice, but knew he needed some lower education.

When his money ran out his friends did too. None came to his aid. He had to hire himself out to a big farmer in that country which sent him into his fields to feed his swine. This wasn't in the Jewish boy's destiny and failed to fit any of his dreams.

He was forced to change his diet due to being destitute, and even the pods he fed the pigs with began to look inviting. His wages must have been minimal and he was falling fast. Fortunately it wasn't too long before he came to himself and realized he and the foreign country were a miss-fit.

The prodigal son came to himself when he realized the swine or country had nothing to do with his destiny, but everything to do with his pride. He knew his father's servants had more bread than they needed, and there he was starving.

Some of us it seems must be awakened by the smelling sauce of broken pride or life before we come to ourselves. Many have made this trip. If a mistake will wake you up and get you saved, God will let it happen. Then you can go back and re-connect with your destiny. It happens. Never forfeit destiny to massage your pride. That will turn into a smelly affair. Discard the places or things that were never meant to be in your destiny while it is in your power to do so.

The young son may have lost his natural wealth but he retained his sense of direction. He knew his father's house was the place to start over. The lessons he had learned about life would cause his love, appreciation, and trust to burn brighter than most. He discarded the misfit.

I will arise and go to my father and say to him, "Father, I have sinned against heaven and before you, and I am no longer worthy to be called your son. Make me like one of your hired servants."—Luke15:18-19

His father had been patiently waiting for this day and embraced his son, and re-connected him with his destiny. He ordered the servants to put the best robe on him, and put a ring on his hand and sandals on his feet, and to kill the fatted calf. It was party time. He said (vs. 24), "For this my son was dead and is alive again; he was lost and is found." And they began to be merry. That fit.

Chapter Thirteen

Refuse to Reason Yourself out of Your Garden

Scores of people have reasoned themselves out of their destiny through entertaining questions and suggestions from Satan and their own flesh. The temptation to wonder into this snare is always sugar coated and sounds reasonable. We need strong faith and discernment to identify and repel these two deadly tactics of the enemy. They are fabricated to defeat us. The more we hear of God's word the stronger our faith grows, and our minds become the assistant of our spirit man and not the instructor.

Some of you may continue to question, "Was it God or emotions in my stomach that I answered that day, or if I was called, am I still called?" If these questions still arouse doubt in you, they need to be settled once and for all so the mind games can cease.

A destined life will unfold naturally as you read God's word, listen to His voice, pray, and submit yourself to capable leaders. Everybody has to be under authority before they're given it. What leader can lead who hasn't been led?

We've established by God's word He has good plans for you, but they seldom develop overnight. Whether you heard Him call you on that particular day or not isn't the real issue. The point of concern is that you hear His call and answer by engaging. He is waiting to confirm what He spoke to you whether it's the second or hundredth time. Your question proves your desire for the truth, and He has it. So ask Him, receive your answer, be at peace and engage.

If you were called, you are called. He hasn't changed His mind. Remember!

For the gifts and callings of God are irrevocable.—Romans 11:29

They can never be withdrawn, but they are subject to change from time to time. I just went through a transition and had to spend more time in prayer than normal to align my spirit with His. I chose to open my mind to His thoughts. I did not ask my mind what it thought. You may have to do the same. It's a common solution to an age old problem. Prayer will unite you with God like nothing else.

We all have questions from time to time, but many originate and are designed by the devil to destroy us. It would benefit us to periodically visit the Garden of Eden to refresh our memory about how man's fall came about.

Satan went to Adam and Eve in their garden with a question, and followed it up with a suggestion.

Now the serpent was more cunning than any beast of the field which the Lord God had made. And he said to the woman, "Has God indeed said, You shall not eat of every tree of the garden?" And the woman said to the serpent, "We may eat the fruit of the trees of the garden; but of the fruit of the tree which is in the midst of the garden, God has said, You shall not eat it, nor shall you touch it, lest you die." Then the serpent said to the woman, "You will not surely die. For God knows that in the day you eat of it your eyes will be opened, and you will be like God, knowing good and evil."—Genesis 3:1-5

They fell for his camouflaged scheme over 5,000 years ago and were driven from their garden. It worked so well it became one of Satan's main stings. If he can deceive you into playing mind games, he can confuse the issues and obstruct justice.

> DECEPTION WILL CAUSE YOUR MIND TO OVERRIDE YOUR SPIRIT MAN AND GIVE REASON THE UPPER HAND.

God calls him a deceiver for a reason. Deception will cause your mind to override your spirit man and give reason the upper hand. The Greater One (Holy Spirit) is in your spirit, not your mind. Our adversary doesn't want to deal with Him. The Holy Spirit will always lead us to use the name of Jesus to quickly cast Satan's lying spirits out of our gardens. Satan and his cohorts are the lessor ones, and must disguise their intent with something that is appealing to our minds.

Jesus has already overcome for us on the cross, and sent the Holy Spirit to dwell in us on the day of Pentecost. There is no power shortage in a Spirit filled Christian.

You are of God, little children, and have overcome them (other lying spirits), because He who is in you is greater than he who is in the world.—1 John 4:4

How then did Satan obtain his goal with Adam and Eve? He came first with a question, "Has God indeed said?" Then he followed it up with a suggestion, "You shall not surely die." He subtly slipped them out of faith with a question that sounded okay. When he had things going his way, he suggested that God didn't really mean what He said. And plus, it would actually improve their lives if they did eat of the fruit of the tree in the midst of their garden. Sound familiar?

Satan transforms himself into an angel of light...11 Corinthians 11:14

Beware of voices that ask you about what God's word really means. That is often an attempt to cast doubt on His word and lure you into transgressing it and feeling okay about doing it. Adam and Eve allowed their minds to override their spirits and reasoned themselves right out of their place, and it happens every day.

Romans 1:17 and Hebrews 10:38 both say, "The just shall live by faith." Hebrews 11:6 adds, "But without faith it is impossible to please Him (God)." And of course Romans 10:17 states, "So then faith comes by hearing, and hearing by the word of God." There is no evidence in the Bible that Christians are to live by human reasoning, but a renewed mind is a must for successful living.

The Bible places much importance and emphasis on our minds. Most of what our five senses gather must pass through and be filtered there. Most of our decisions are made in our minds, and we are to value, use and protect it. That is why it so important to follow God's word concerning it.

And do not be conformed to this world, but be transformed by the renewing of your mind, that you may prove what is that good and acceptable and perfect will (word) of God.—Romans 12:2

The will of God is the written and spoken word of God. His will is His word. Our minds are to be transformed (cross over and be formed) by God's word after we are born again. Then they will work in unity with and complement our born-again spirits. We will avoid many snares and mistakes when our minds are in agreement with our spirits. How can two walk together unless they agree?

> GOD GAVE US A MIND AND HE EXPECTS US TO DEVELOP AND USE IT THROUGHOUT LIFE.

God gave us a mind and He expects us to develop and use it throughout life. It is part of our make-up and who we are. The mind is a wonderful and complex thing. We are to educate it and stretch it daily to keep it active.

But the fact remains; the language in the Kingdom of God is faith. The word of the Lord endures forever, and will not change. Satan is aware of that, and the power of God's word spoken from the lips of His children. He must cloud the issue with a question to get us to bite on his suggestions. If he can lure us out of faith, he will not have to confront the Greater One in our spirits. If he can con us into reasoning about what God said, like it or not, the issue will become cloudy.

When reasoning has replaced faith, the opportunity is conducive to suggest a half-truth (lie). The half-truth has become believable because faith is absent and the lie sounds reasonable.

Many Christians get snared in this ageless scheme. Their enemy (and often flesh too) draws them away from faith by what sounds, looks, feels, smells, or tastes good. They think all is well and take a bite of it. Then their eyes are opened and they realize how naked they are without their covering of faith (which is their trust in God and His word).

They yielded to the temptation when they thought everything sounded reasonable. When they sinned, they ran and hid from God, but He loved them and us too much to leave them there. He found them as He does us and clothed them as He does us with His forgiveness. However, they had to leave their garden (their destined place).

Thank God we are living in the dispensation of grace! Many of us have had to leave our gardens of destiny after a fall, but were allowed to re-enter after true repentance.

> **If he will try to use the scheme on Jesus, nobody is exempt.**

Adam and Eve went on and populated the earth, but paid severely for their sin. Thank God we can move on too, and scars are good reminders of how crafty questions and suggestions can cut into our futures.

When the enemy questioned Eve, Adam should have gotten in his face and answered with power: "God said it and that settles it! Get out of here."

Satan isn't a creator, he's only a re-runner

He even tried this same trick on Jesus after He had fasted for forty days in the wilderness (he waits for a weak moment). He then questioned Jesus' deity and suggested He prove it. In Matthew 4:3 the tempter had the nerve to say, "If You are the Son of God, command that these stones become bread." If he will try to use the scheme on Jesus, nobody is exempt.

After feeding 5,000 with a boy's lunch, it would not have been a problem for Jesus, but that wasn't the issue. The issue was not to be drawn into conversing with the devil. Yes, Jesus was hungry, but He wasn't about to be conned out of His faith by giving way to reason, or let His stomach make the decision.

He nor we owe the tempter any kind of proof of anything except who we are in Christ Jesus by replying with God's word. In the next verse Jesus gave Satan all the answer he deserved. He said in verse 4: "It is written, Man shall not live by bread alone, but by every word that proceeds from the mouth of God." His faith and discernment repelled the temptation to allow reasoning into the equation.

God told me once, "You have become too passive with the devil. Your quietness is his consent." I replied, "Yes Sir, You are correct, I will change my attitude toward him immediately." I did and have become very vocal in prayer and decreeing God's word since. We must let the enemy and our flesh, know where we stand, or we may not be there long.

We never find Jesus being passive with the devil. He triumphed over him repeatedly with the power of God's word. He kept the issues clear and on the table, and we must do the same. He never allowed human reasoning to give the answer, and He is our example. How was He able to do this?

I believe much of His ability came from His prayer life. In the Gospels we find Him praying often, praying all night, praying earnestly, and even vehemently. He built up His faith by praying in and by the leadership of the Holy Spirit. His faith remained sufficient to identify and resist the questions and suggestions aimed at His destiny.

His enemies or flesh never succeeded in their invitations for Him to play their mind games. He functioned in faith, not reason, and He never failed.

When Jesus' earthly ministry was coming to an end, tremendous pressure came upon Him to reason Himself out of His ultimate destiny. He was deeply distressed in His garden of Gethsemane, but by the help of the Holy Spirit, He said to His Father; "Not My will, but Thine be done." Then He went on to the cross and finished delivering His earthly destiny. Where would you and I be if He hadn't?

Refuse to be fooled! Know who is for you and who is against you

The enemy will question you about the accuracy of God's written word as well as His spoken word to you. When he does, he's fishing for your faith. If you converse with him, he is setting his hook. Stop him now with "It is written" or whatever he suggests will sound reasonable.

> **When an enemy comes into your space and questions you about God's word concerning your destiny, make no mistake, it's time for war.**

When an enemy comes into your space and questions you about God's word concerning your destiny, make no mistake, it's time for war. For though we walk in the flesh, we do not war according to the flesh; for the weapons of our warfare are not carnal (of the flesh) but mighty in God for pulling down strongholds.

2 Corinthians 10:3-4 reminds us we're in a spiritual war and must use our mighty spiritual weapons in and of God to win it. We must handle the deceivers with the sword of the Spirit to stay in our places. Reasoning about what they say often gives them their way.

The thief does not come except to steal, and to kill, and to destroy. I (Jesus) have come that they (us) may have life, and that they may have it more abundantly.—John 10:10

There are only three things on our enemy's mind. When he attempts to lure you away from God's word or your destiny, he has three ambitions. They never change! No matter how reasonable his questions sound or how wonderful his suggestions seem, behind the two, lies a deadly scheme. He wants to steal, kill, or destroy the life and destiny that Jesus came for you to have.

> WHEN "IT IS WRITTEN IN THE WORD OF GOD" COMES OUT OF THE MOUTH OF A CHRISTIAN, HELL TREMBLES AND INTRUDERS DISPERSE.

It matters little to our enemy how he takes us down. What really matters is that he does it before we become God's servants and enter our true destinies. We become a serious foe then, and his chances for victory are marginal. He well understands the Greater One is in us, and when we turn Him lose, we win.

Make no mistake, our enemy is well organized and can be as smooth as silk. Remember how he cunningly caused Israel to wander in the wilderness forty years. After all the miracles those ten spies had seen God perform, and after they even beheld their majestic promised place for forty days, giants slithered into their heads. They were willing to leave them there, and it mattered little what God said. All they could think about then was giants, giants and more giants. They in turn passed that mindset on to others and it caused over 500,000 deaths and prolonged a nation from entering their destiny for forty long grueling years.

When anybody or anything begins to magnify what may be against what God has for you, beware and be wise, it is often a disguise. At that time, God usually has a door open for you. Any decision to move forward with God will unlock the provision and invite the protection of God.

It is the Greater One in us that will discern and repel with power the temptations that come our way. When "It is written in the word of God" comes out of the mouth of a Christian, hell trembles and intruders disperse.

For whatever is born of God overcomes (defeats) the world. And this is the victory that has overcome the world—our faith (in the work & word of Christ).— 1John 5:4

If whatever dream, call, service, or idea you have is born of God, it will overcome the adversity against it. In fact, our faith in the work and word of Jesus Christ has already defeated what opposes us. However, it is foolish to expect a trouble free life when serious about your future in God. You must be willing to stand against the schemes of the enemy, and keep standing and praying till he flees from your garden. The Greater One in you will empower you to do so.

That will clear the way for you to move forward with your destiny.

Chapter Fourteen

The Dreamer

"Lord, why didn't You just send Mrs. Potiphar away that day? I wouldn't be in this terrible place if You had only stepped in with a grain of help." Joseph was in a cold dark prison cell, and it didn't make any sense to him at all. This failed to fall in line with his dreams again. How quickly he was robbed of a favored position a second time. Life had dealt him another bad hand. There was no truth in her yells of injustice, and he failed to see why the tables of destiny had turned so abruptly again.

"Why did the Potiphar house have to be as empty as it was that day? And where did she get the nerve to grab my garment so tight I had to leave it in her hands to escape?" She had asked Joseph time and time again to sleep with her, but he had refused her every effort. He had told her it was wrong and he could not sin against his God. "Why couldn't she understand?"

He had even purposely kept his distance from the lady of the house due to the wanton look in her eyes for him daily. He guessed she resented him for saying no.

The unanswered questions punctured him like a dull knife. They also brought back vivid memories of the pit his brothers threw him in because of their resentment. It had struck again, but what would be his fate this time?

His dreams and the coat of many colors that his father Jacob had given him had charted only a harsh course full of tragedy so far. After escaping death from the first pit, he had fared far better than most. They had threatened to let him die there, but changed their minds when they saw a caravan of camels in the distance.

It turned out to be a band of Ishmaelite traders headed to Egypt with goods and spices to sell. His scheming brothers thought, "Why shed innocent blood when you can sell it and make money instead." So they pulled him out of the pit and struck a deal with the Midianite traders. They sold Joseph for twenty pieces of silver and watched him and the merchants disappear in a cloud of dust toward Egypt.

He never dreamed he would be thrown into another pit, but the damp and musky smell of the prison cell proved different. He soberly determined that things couldn't get much worse, and drifted off to sleep that first night in the dungeon.

Joseph the Dreamer

Jacob had twelve sons and the eleventh one is the only recorded dreamer in the variegated bunch. It doesn't matter where you fall in the birth line, if you're the one that dreams, you're the one that leads.

> LIKE MANY OF US AT ONE TIME OR ANOTHER JOSEPH WAS AT ANOTHER PLACE OF SEVERE TESTING.

Like many of us at one time or another Joseph was at another place of severe testing. What would he do now? Would what God told him in dreams be enough to provide the fire and light needed in a cold dark prison?

With the dreams he had been given earlier, Joseph knew he was destined for something great. In his dreams, his entire family was bowing down to him, which was an inclination that all would serve under him one day. Plus his father had favored him above all his brothers by giving him a special coat. That set the stage for a double feature of jealousy and resentment before the dreams ever came into the picture.

Now Israel (Jacob) loved Joseph more than all his children, because he was the son of his old age. Also he made him a tunic of many colors. But when his brothers saw that their father loved him more than all his brothers, they hated him and could not speak peaceably to him. ----Genesis 37:3-4

The family was splintered with indignation for father's preferred one already. I can't understand Jacob flaunting his affections even more for his beloved Joseph so openly. It is a serious mistake to favor certain ones in a family, but displaying his fondness so blatantly humiliated and infuriated his other sons. Had he lost his sense fatherhood?

The brothers had enough to deal with already, and were being stretched beyond the norm with disregard. Then Joseph began to dream and added insult to their wounded feelings.

Now Joseph had a dream, and he told it to his brothers; and they hated him even more. So he said to them, "Please hear this dream which I have dreamed: There we were, binding sheaves (bundles of grain) in the field. Then behold, my sheaf arose and also stood upright; and indeed your sheaves stood all around and bowed down to my sheaf." And his brothers said to him, "Shall you indeed reign over us? Or shall you indeed have dominion over us?" So they hated him even more for his dreams and for his words.—Genesis 37:5-8

Only a carnival of events could happen after such an elaborate and detailed description of how his brothers would bow down and serve him one day. They were on fire with hate, but somehow Joseph was willing to take his presentations to another level. Had his dreams blinded him to the point he couldn't see his brother's disdain? It seemed it had. It can happen to us too.

Then he dreamed still another dream and told it to his brothers, and said "Look, I have dreamed another dream. And this time, the sun, the moon, and the eleven stars bowed down to me." So he told it to his father and his brothers; and his father rebuked him and said to him, "What is this dream that you have dreamed? Shall your mother and I and your brothers indeed come to bow down to the earth before you?" And his brothers envied him, but his father kept the matter in mind. — Genesis 37:9-11

You might say this put the bitter icing on the obnoxious cake that nobody ever wanted baked in the first place. How dare the boy to open the second act more repulsive than the first. How offensive could the boy get? Father and mother were now looking up to him in his dreams. It appeared both wheels on the apple cart of Jacob's family just ran off.

Did you notice that Joseph never asked anyone if they wanted to hear about his dreams? He just supposed they would. This should be a lesson to us all. When we willingly announce to those close by how great our dreams are, we're rolling out the red carpet for trouble.

Joseph told his dreams as a teenage boy too full of himself to question the Lord on how any of his dreams would be fulfilled or where. How it all would come about and how long it would take probably never entered his mind. Most of us have been in his shoes, and can relate to his mistakes.

Being only seventeen or so, he didn't expect it would take long. Someone would notice he was special by the beautiful robe he wore that his father had made for him. He would catch the eye of a man of wealth or position and then his character would speak for itself. A title and status awaited him just around the corner. Then his family would look up to him. What else could happen? He hadn't constructed the dreams. God gave them to him.

> GOD HAD GONE DEEP-SEA FISHING WITH
> SOME VERY LIVE DREAM BAIT.

Joseph understood precisely what his dreams meant. Jacob had taught the boy well, but was perplexed when Joseph told him that he too would be bowing and looking up to him. What kind of thing was that to say to a Jewish father that had endured so much? Humiliating his brothers was enough to cause plenty of rifts in the family as it was.

His father thought that maybe the coat he had given the boy had gone to his head. "He is my favorite and most prized son, but he sure has been acting strange lately with all his dreams," Jacob thought. He hoped his son was okay and would calm down, so there could be a measure of peace in the family again. He regretted giving him the robe. "Does the boy think he is to take my place?" His father wondered about the dreams, but could make little sense of them.

I must admit and believe you also have had dreams about being a hero. However, if I had told my dad he would be bowing to me one day, he would probably have took more action than just wondering what my dreams meant.

To say that Joseph was bold is an understatement. But then how could one so young handle such a hook in his mouth? God had gone deep-sea fishing with some very live dream bait. He had hooked the one that could handle the highest position, but he had to be highly tested.

He would give him plenty of line and sit back and watch the show. Would he shake the hook out of his jaw and swim away or would he allow God to slowly reel him in?

Yes! I believe God enjoys watching us swim around with His hook in our mouths. I'm sure He's laughed at me a few times when I tried to pull against His line. I was free entertainment. What father doesn't get pleasure from watching his children grow up? "Kids are quite entertaining." Or should I say "we are quite entertaining?"

When Joseph was given plenty of line, he acted like the rest of us would at seventeen. He could hardly contain himself, and swam around his brothers recounting his dreams. The fish sang like a bird, but his dreams stung like a bee. His brothers were extremely offended by father's pet and his multi-colored coat.

The brothers were seething while Joseph sounded like he was teasing. Resentment was building and the temperature was rising in the very dysfunctional family.

When God sets His hook in us, it causes a change in our character. We may act a little wild, loud, or out of control, especially when we're young. Who among us could keep quiet with such dreams at that age? Not me.

Keeping quiet is something we're not accustomed to. It's almost impossible to accomplish it, but we all need to work on it and God knows it. What we often forget to grasp is the hook is just the conception period. It's like embarking on a trip. There is a distance between departure and arrival to which we tend to give little thought. I even catch myself wanting to ignore it.

When we travel on vacation for any distance we are guaranteed to come upon road construction, detours and heavy slow traffic. It's the in-between that wears on us.

Having God's hook in our jaw is far superior to being eaten by sharks, but doesn't mean we're capable of conducting Kingdom business yet.

Joseph dreamed dreams that would not come true for many years. Did he think his family was ready to follow the young leader? I doubt it. He was so young and excited he just had to announce it to his closest company. They were not impressed with father's favorite, and they began to hate him for his dreams. The day and opportunity arrived one day to rid themselves of both. His brothers had been tending their father's flock in a pasture at Shechem for quite a while. Jacob had sent Joseph there to check on them, but they had moved on by the time he got there. He was wandering around looking for them when a man of that area noticed him.

The man asked him what he was looking for, and he told him his brothers. The man replied that he had overheard them saying they were going on to Dothan. So Joseph journeyed on toward there and saw them in the distance.

Now when they saw him afar off, even before he came near them, they conspired against him to kill him. Then they said to one another, "Look, this dreamer is coming! "Come therefore, let us now kill him and cast him into some pit; and we shall say, Some wild beast has devoured him. We shall see what will become of his dreams!"—Genesis 37:18-20

The eldest brother Reuben had secretly planned to come back to the pit and rescue Joseph, but while he was away the Ishmaelite caravan had come by. Another brother, Judah, didn't want to shed innocent family blood either, so he came up with the idea of selling Joseph to the Ishmaelites who were Midianite traders.

When the merchants got to Egypt they sold Joseph to Potiphar, an Egyptian officer of Pharaoh, and captain of his guard. Mr. Potiphar had no small title and much fell on his shoulders. He had little time to handle his personal affairs or business interests.

Joseph had long been stripped of his beautiful robe, but Potiphar saw something in the young man that caused him to believe he was trustworthy. Some would venture to think at this point that God had left the dreamer's side, but not so.

The Lord was with Joseph, and he was a successful man; and he was in the house of his master the Egyptian. And his master saw that the Lord was with him and that the Lord made all he did to prosper in his hand. So

Joseph found favor in his sight, and served him. Then he made him overseer of his house, and all that he had he put under his authority.—Genesis 39:2-4

Everything Potiphar owned or had interest in had been turned over to Joseph. The Bible says in the next two verses that everything about Potiphar's house was blessed because of Joseph. Whether it was business in his house or in the field, it was blessed of the Lord. It came to a point where Mr. Potiphar didn't even know what he had except for the food that he ate.

Joseph had served him well and he knew the hand of God was upon his affairs because of the now young Hebrew man. He could focus his attentions on his Palace position and have some free time now that Joseph was managing all his house and business interests. Life had improved immensely since adding the Hebrew.

I believe it distressed Potiphar severely when his wife accused Joseph of trying to rape her. I further believe he was very suspicious of his wife's accusations, but was forced to have Joseph cast into prison to save her reputation. To me, sparing his servant's life proved he was aware of his innocence. It would have taken little effort to have him executed if he so desired.

While Joseph was sitting in prison those first few days, not any of the pieces to his puzzle of life seemed to fit anywhere. The prison was as odious as some people that had been in his life, but he was determined he'd made the right decision not to lay with his master's wife.

HE HAD NO WAY OF KNOWING YET THAT
MR. POTIPHAR'S HOUSE WAS ONLY A PLACE
OF LEARNING HOW TO HANDLE MONEY AND
RECKLESS WOMEN.

He had no way of knowing yet that Mr. Potiphar's house was only a place of learning how to handle money and reckless women. He went to prison in spite of being successful on both issues. No, God had not forsaken him this time either.

Joseph simply had passed his tests at Potiphar's house and was being promoted in a contrary way. The way up with God again usually takes a dip down first. Joseph was so busy tending to Potiphar's affairs and dodging his wife's intentions, he hadn't had the peace of mind to dream much. He needed to practice up for the future, and unbeknown to him, a couple of prospects were headed his way.

The Lord continued to be with Joseph and showed him mercy and gave him favor with the keeper of the prison. Pretty soon, the keeper perceived the hand of the Lord was upon Joseph and like Potiphar, he turned everything over to him. The prison was completely under the hand of Joseph's authority. Whatever he did there, the Lord blessed. God may not work in our lives like we think He will or should, but He works for us.

It came to pass after these things that the butler and the baker of the King of Egypt offended their Lord, the King of Egypt. And Pharaoh was angry with his

two officers, the chief butler and the chief baker. So
he put them in custody in the house of the captain of
the guard, in the prison, the place where Joseph was
confined.—Genesis 40:1-3

The butler and the baker, of course, came directly under the
supervision of Joseph while they were there. It just so happened
that they both had a dream on the same night in prison. When
he saw them the next morning they both looked depressed so
Joseph asked them what was wrong.

They said to him (vs. 8) "We each have had a dream, and
there is no interpreter of it." So Joseph said to them, "Do not
interpretations belong to God? Tell them to me, please."

The chief butler went first and told his dream. Joseph told
him the interpretation of his dream was that in three days Pharaoh would lift him out prison and restore him to his position.
He asked the butler to please make mention of him to Pharaoh
to get him out of the dungeon, for he was innocent of all charges
against him.

When the baker saw that the interpretation Joseph gave
sounded good, he told him his dream. The baker was not to fare
so well. Joseph told him the interpretation of his dream was that
in three days Pharaoh would lift him from prison also, but would
hang him.

In three days it happened to both men just as Joseph had
interpreted their dreams. The chief butler was restored and the
chief baker was hanged.

Yet the chief butler did not remember Joseph, but forgot him.—Genesis 40:23

However, God did not. After two full years had passed, He gave Pharaoh a very disturbing dream about fat cows and skinny cows. Pharaoh called for all his magicians and wise men but none could give him peace by interpreting his dream. He is disgruntled and disgusted with the lot of them. They were supposed to be capable interpreters.

The chief butler witnessed the chaos in the Palace and the frustration of the King, and remembered his fault. He had forgotten about Joseph! He then went to Pharaoh and informed him about Joseph and how he had perfectly interpreted the chief baker's and his dreams.

Pharaoh sent for Joseph and they brought him out of the dungeon quickly. He shaved, changed his clothing, and went before the King. The King said, "I have had a dream and there is no one who can interpret it. But I have heard it said of you that you can understand a dream to interpret it."

So Joseph answered Pharaoh, saying, "It is not in me; God will give Pharaoh an answer of peace."—Genesis 41:16

Joseph told the King the truth and made him feel special with one brief statement. God was going to give Pharaoh peace of mind by giving him the interpretation.

The King enlightens Joseph of his dream about how seven fine looking cows came up out of the river and fed in the meadow. And then seven of the poorest, ugliest, and gaunt looking cows he had ever seen came up and ate the first seven fat cows. But they didn't look any better afterward than before.

Then he told him about the seven heads of grain that came up on one stalk, and then how seven withered, thin, and blighted by the east wind sprang up and devoured them.

Then Joseph said to Pharaoh, "The dreams of Pharaoh are one; God has shown Pharaoh what He is about to do: The seven good cows are seven years, and the seven good heads are seven years; the dreams are one. And the seven thin and ugly cows which came up after them are seven years, and the seven empty heads blighted by the east wind are seven years of famine."—Genesis 41:25-27

Joseph went on to tell the King that God was about to send seven years of great plenty throughout all the land of Egypt. But they would be followed by seven years of famine so severe that the seven good years would be forgotten about completely.

Joseph advised Pharaoh to select a discerning and wise man and set him over the land of Egypt. Let him appoint officers to collect one fifth of all the produce of the land in the seven plentiful years. Let it be stored under the authority of Pharaoh in different cities, so that the land of Egypt wouldn't perish during the severe famine. His advice sounded good to Pharaoh and all his servants.

And Pharaoh said to his servants, "Can we find such a one as this, a man in whom is the Spirit of God?" Then Pharaoh said to Joseph, "Inasmuch as God has shown you all of this, there is no one as discerning and wise as you. You shall be over my house, and all my people shall be ruled according to your word; only in regard to the throne will I be greater than you." —Genesis 41:38-40

God revealed a truth to me years ago in the life of Joseph in which many of you are aware. If a God given gift or dream lands you in some sort of jail, stay with your gift and keep dreaming, they are what will lift you back out. Joseph's dreams had a major role in his descending, but had everything to do with his ascending.

IF A GOD GIVEN GIFT OR DREAM LANDS YOU IN SOME SORT OF JAIL, STAY WITH YOUR GIFT AND KEEP DREAMING, THEY ARE WHAT WILL LIFT YOU BACK OUT.

Loyal hearts and faith are what God continually searches for. Man's method is to inspect the exterior, but the Lord has x-ray vision. He's interested with what's inside us. Joseph had the credentials God was seeking to save nations.

Joseph was thirty years old when he stood before Pharaoh King of Egypt. And Joseph went out from the presence of Pharaoh, and went throughout all the land of Egypt.—Genesis 41:46

He was around seventeen when his brothers sold him to the Midianite merchants. Few people make it to his position in a life time, much less in thirteen years.

Joseph could talk to Kings like no other, and Pharaoh couldn't have made a better choice than to select him to manage the enormous fourteen-year task. The seven years of plenty were good as God had said, and the seven years of famine were proving to be as severe.

So when all the land of Egypt was famished, the people cried to Pharaoh for bread. Then Pharaoh said to all the Egyptians, "Go to Joseph; whatever he says to you, do."—Genesis 41:55

Joseph was the overseer of all the grain sold during the famine. It became so severe that all the countries around Egypt, including Canaan became victims of the famine. All were coming to Joseph in Egypt for grain.

Joseph is about thirty-nine now and hasn't seen or heard from his family in about twenty-two years, but a famine could remedy that. Hard times seem to pull families together.

When Joseph's father Jacob heard that there was grain in Egypt he scolded his sons. He asked them why they were sitting around just looking at one another, and ordered them to go to Egypt and buy grain before they all died. It seemed they still had an issue or two even with the dreamer out of their hair. What was their problem now? Yes, they would be at the mercy of the Egyptians, but it would be better than watching their families starve. The boys resented the dreamer, but fact is they needed him desperately. None of them dreamed.

Now Joseph was governor over the land; and it was he who sold to all the people of the land. And Joseph's brothers came and bowed down before him with their faces to the earth.—Genesis 42:6

Joseph then recognized his brothers, but he was using an Egyptian name and made up like one so they failed to distinguish who he was. He also spoke roughly to them to further hide his identity. He asked them where they were from and, of course, they told him Canaan.

Then Joseph remembered the dreams which he had dreamed about them, and said to them, "You are spies! You have come to see the nakedness of the land!" And they said to him, "No, my lord, but your servants have come to buy food. We are all one man's sons, we are honest men; your servants are not spies."—Genesis 42:9-11

It was most difficult for Joseph to remain unknown to his brothers their first visit, but he managed. The famine was only into its second year and his brothers would have to come back if their families were to survive.

When they returned the second time, he could not hold back any longer. He saw that God was behind all of his brothers' decisions so that their family and nation wouldn't be erased from the earth by the famine.

He wept upon his brothers' shoulders as he identified himself. I believe he wept for them, but more so for the goodness of God to position him in such a place to preserve their lives as well as thousands more.

"But now, do not therefore be grieved or angry with yourselves because you sold me here, for God sent me before you to preserve life. For these two years the famine has been in the land, and there are still five years in which there will be neither plowing nor harvesting. And God sent me before you to preserve a posterity for you in the earth, and to save your lives by a great deliverance."—Genesis 45:5-7

Many years and events took place between Joseph's dreams and the time when his brothers bowed down before him to save their lives.

If God gives you impossible sounding dreams, stay faithful to the Lord. For on your destiny, many may cling.

Chapter Fifteen

Make Room for Your Destiny

It doesn't matter who you are or where you come from, what you learn or laugh at in this chapter will be worth the price of the book. Fiction has no mastery over fact when we submit to the truth.

It is nothing short of amazing the emphasis we ascribe to our wants until they become our haves. The new car that smelled like leather three months ago smells like French fries now. A style lasts about as long as a smile. Much of what is advertised as new and improved will soon be marked down and removed.

My wife wanted to walk in the mornings to build up her energy without being weather hindered. No problem! There were dozens of used treadmills for sale, but I wasn't about to skimp on this purchase. I bought her a brand new one. I forget what brand it was, but wow, it was a miracle worker. She only had to use it three times. I spent more time in assembling than she did exercising. It's gone.

We have a sixty-five acre tree farm where you can find me restoring my soul when it's convenient, and sometimes when it's not. I have a large tractor because I'm a half-day warrior and like plenty of horsepower. The few implements needed for my small operation were bought with the tractor years ago. However, I convinced myself last year a different plow was needed more than my next meal. I had to have it! Found a good used one, paid the man, and he fork-lifted it onto my trailer. When I got to my little tree farm, reality set in. There was no forklift there, or man waiting to drive it. That was just the beginning of my sorrows.

> WHEN YOU ARE WILLING TO ADMIT
> YOU MADE A MISTAKE, THEN AND ONLY
> THEN CAN YOU CUT YOURSELF AWAY
> FROM IT AND MOVE ON.

I went into my innovative role, and miraculously got that plow off the trailer, and am still living. I gave my used plow a new name and that's about all you need to know about that.

Once off and after much heartache, it was finally attached to my Big Ben, and I bee-lined to plow our wildlife food plots. Fifty percent of my used plow's luster was already gone. The other fifty was about to go! I was distraught at how this thousand-pound piece-of-junk iron butchered my neat parcels. I'm sure the wildlife thought "take it back!" It already needs a new home. Don't even like to look at it now. The thing has zero appeal at present and it is going.

I confessed to you earlier of not being the sharpest knife in the drawer, but a knife I am. When you are willing to admit you made a mistake, then and only then can you cut yourself away from it and move on. I made my decision long ago not to die strangled by attachments.

Therefore we also, since we are surrounded by so great a cloud of witnesses, let us lay aside every weight, and the sin which so easily ensnares us, and let us run with endurance the race that is set before us.—Hebrews 12:1

If we are to run with our Lord (or move with our destiny) we must lay aside some weights and sins. Notice how none are excluded; let us lay aside every weight. If you are think you haven't any, you are only fooling yourself. They come in all sizes and shapes, and some even hide in our minds. The unseen ones can be the toughest to identify and toss aside.

I have less trouble giving up objects than opinions. How we view our things and thoughts determines whether we cut lose and follow on, or fall away.

> ALMOST EVERY TIME GOD LEADS US ON,
> WE USUALLY HAVE TO LEAVE
> SOMETHING BEHIND.

Hebrews 4:12 states, "For the word of God is living and powerful, and sharper than any two-edged sword, piercing even unto the division of soul and spirit, and of joints and marrow, and is a discerner of the thoughts and intents of the heart."

The apostle Paul is informing us that God's word is sharp enough to cut away things, thoughts and intents that will hinder us from running with our Lord in obedience.

Almost every time God leads us on, we usually have to leave something behind. When He offers us more, we have the decision to make room for it or allow it to pass on. This scripture is not just about money only. Please be flexible.

"Give, and it will be given to you: good measure, pressed down, shaken together, and running over will be put into your bosom. For with the same measure that you use, it will be measured back to you."—Luke 6:38

When we used to wrestle as kids we'd try to grab the other in some kind of position and ask, "Do you give up?" If we said yes, we were let go free. We had to give up our will to fight on and turn loose of what we held to. If we said, "I give up" there was a process of exchange that took place, and we were let go.

When God said to whoever gives, more will be given; He had an exchange in mind also. He was implying that if we would give up something (weight, sin, room, thought, etc.) more of what He had to offer would be given to us.

It would be helpful for us to identify sin as anything that separates us from God. It can be good things as well as bad. Laying aside a bad thing for a good one is a no brainer. Turning loose of a good thing for better is a horse of a different color. But if God is holding two birds in the bush which belong to me, the cage door to my one must be opened.

Many have much on the ball but still miss their destiny call. When our stuff, no matter the description, begins to weight us down and control us, we just got outsourced. We see this happen in the next scripture.

Now behold, one came and said to Him, "Good Teacher, what good thing shall I do that I may have eternal life?"—Matthew 19:16

Jesus told him if he wanted to enter into life (his real destiny) he needed to keep the commandments. This guy was used to negotiating business deals so he pushed the issue and revealed his cards. "Which ones?" he asked. Like many, he was used to picking and choosing. No problem – Jesus tossed out the six that dealt with the exterior part of man. The young man, in self-justification, replied he'd been practicing those since he was a boy. He wanted to know what he still lacked. He knew he was missing something.

Jesus said to him, "If you want to be perfect," (whole or mature) "go sell what you have and give to the poor, and you will have treasure in heaven; and come follow Me."—Matthew 19:21

The next verse says, "When the young man heard that saying, he went away sorrowful, for he had great possessions."

"Mr. Successful, wait a minute, back up. Listen longer! Ask another question, and let that offer sink in. He's only asked twelve more in the whole world to follow Him. You're walking away from your destiny."

"He didn't tell you to give all your money to the poor either." He said, "give to the poor!" "Mr. Successful, get those great possessions out of your ears. They're causing you great problems. Give up something and make room for your destiny. You have a full house, but it's a losing hand." Nothing turned him. He outsourced himself. He refused to make room for his destiny.

The Bible doesn't even give this guy a name. He could be anybody. He's described as young and wealthy, but not wise and healthy. He's like some you know. He seems to have gotten a handle on life early and did well in business or was brought up with a silver spoon in mouth. The Bible doesn't say.

There is an old saying that if you don't want to know the truth, then you should have enough sense not to ask for it. If you deem your possessions more valuable than your purpose, why show your laundry?

Another replacement for Judas must be found. This guy's house and bank account seemed to be full, and he refused to give up any room! He allowed his things and status to choke out the destiny he seemingly had been prepared for. He drifted off the pages of the Bible much quieter than he came on and was never heard from again. He was in perfect position, but refused to make room for his destiny.

And God says, "Okay, next!"

Be Willing to Down-Size to Move Up

Several years ago my wife and I were living in Thomasville, GA, and driving to Tallahassee, FL to attend church. We were very involved there so decided to sell our home in Thomasville and move thirty miles south to the northern outskirts of Tallahassee. Our house sold soon and we moved into a rental until we built, and then moved into our new four-bedroom home.

Two years later my dad started having issues with his legs, and he needed help just to get in and out of bed. He was in his eighties at the time, and I wanted to do what I could to help. That would require another move. My folks lived in Cairo, GA.

So we sold our new spacious four-bedroom house that we had just furnished two years prior. Bought an older two bedroom tight house on the east side of Cairo, which was only thirteen miles from Thomasville where we both were still in business. Then we faced the unachievable.

It is irrelevant how hard you try or how witty you are, the furniture out of a modern four-bedroom house will not fit in an older tight two-bedroom home. Something had to go, and I mean a lot of somethings. We had to make room!

We had a large spacious kitchen with the latest turntable type storage and plenty of room for a breakfast table, chairs, and a snack bar. Now there was a path with a spot for a table and two chairs and very little cabinet space. We bought this house years ago and still haven't a clue where some of our stuff is. My wife has complained about fruit dishes and Christmas decorations for almost eight years. My humble and only answer is, "I don't know where they are. They must be in our storage somewhere."

I couldn't be completely honest with her, but after a few years I forgot what I was looking for. I'm not into dishes and décor too much anyway. I'd rather be at my little cabin hide-away on the hill having fun with my grandson Jackson and granddaughter Anna Kate.

I guess you want to know what we kept and what we stored. That one is easy! We kept what we needed, some of the best, and let go of the rest! We gave away, threw away, lost some, and stored what was left.

After doing without many of our items for a while, we forgot them. That is except for those fruit dishes and that stuffed snowman. I couldn't see what was so special about that guy, but we discuss him every December. I believe it was just too hot for him in that south GA storage and he moved north. I have to answer the same questions every December about that deserter.

> BOTTOM LINE IS THAT IF YOU PLAN
> TO MOVE WITH DESTINY, YOU'LL
> HAVE TO *MAKE ROOM* FOR IT.

Bottom line is that if you plan to move with destiny, you'll have to *make room* for it. It was not the smartest looking thing we ever did, but it was the right thing. I needed to be in the area where we moved to handle some things, and I was able to help with my Dad too.

The motto of our experience is that too many are trying to force a four-bedroom life in a two-bedroom week. Something has got to go! Many people can't move on with their destinies because they're weighted down with too many material goods and fruitless responsibilities. If we fail to make room for our destinies, we will get squeezed out of our potential.

When destiny knocks on your door, it is vital you make room for it. It may not come back for a while! The Lord will help you toss aside heavy things, thoughts, habits or places to make room for your destiny when you give the signal.

You can be at the right place at the right time with all the right people and still miss your destiny if you're unwilling to make room for it.

Nothing we own is more valuable than what God is trying to give us. Who can out-give God?

Chapter Sixteen

Miracles Require Movement, Just Do It

At the time of this encounter with the Lord, I had been praying for people in a certain region for about three years. My wife and I had been invited by two other couples to join them in prayer in the same vicinity and we accepted. The Lord just knitted us together for a while in intercession for that particular area and people.

After a year or so of prayer, we hosted an outdoor concert for them and provided roasted hotdogs and drinks. These people were on our hearts and we just wanted to interact with and do something for them.

I met a pastor who had recently built a church close to the same area, and it was a divine connection from the word go. He was a commercial pilot and I knew the company he flew for out of Tallahassee, FL, and personally knew the owner as well. I

wanted to base my ministry as close to that region as possible
and this was about as good as it could get. He had an extra office,
so we struck a deal. I helped him with the church and services
and filled in for him when he was out of town. He was very
gracious to me in return and helped me with a new office and
use of the church facility. It was one of those win-win situations.

Months passed and I continued praying for the area along
with Mr. Potter, my new prayer partner. Then out of the blue, the
Lord spoke to me one Saturday while I was alone at home. He
said, "Hold a week long revival on the south side of town where
you are." I guess the surprise on my face said it all, because He
added, "You have no excuse not to."

How could I argue? He was right. I was already holding one
and two-night meetings there, so upon His word I started calling
friends to help me. God loves to get you in those positions where
you have to eat crow to say no.

I needed a worship leader to assemble a diverse praise team
quickly, so called my good friend, Stina Brockman. Our families have been close friends for almost fifteen years, and we've
worked together several times. She accepted the invitation and
put together the praise team and musicians.

The Lord directed me to allow younger speakers to preach
half of the time, and I'm aware that is somewhat risky. But when
God has you where He wants you, all you can say is, "Yes Sir."
The whole team was a great mixture of people and in less than
ten days we were holding revival.

After the first week, we went for another, and then scaled it back to Tuesday nights only for several more weeks before ending it.

After the meetings, my prayer partner Mr. Potter and I sensed we were to keep interceding for the area and the people, so we continued.

Almost a year passed and I hadn't received any promptings to hold more meetings, so began to speak some locally. Another church also began holding services in the same church where I was and needed space. Since I wasn't holding meetings, I was more than obliged to step aside.

I had stepped down from my positions at church due to being absent on Sunday mornings and others had stepped up. Mr. Potter and I at this point were only meeting in the area to pray. I am telling you this for a reason.

> ## WHEN GOD SAYS "NOW" HE
> ### DOESN'T MEAN NEXT WEEK.

We were at our weekly prayer meeting praying for the same people and region when something unusual happened. Suddenly, God spoke to me, and to my surprise He said, "I'm lifting this burden from you now." I journal most of His directions so immediately wrote down the date, time, and message. When God says "now" He doesn't mean next week.

I had no loose ends to tie up, no staff to disband, and nothing to hinder me from obeying the Lord immediately. The two of us had been interceding alone for almost a year in the area after I had closed the meetings. For clarity I want to say again, "I had no loose ends to tie up."

In such cases, and it may not happen very often, we are obligated to turn loose, let go and move on. Please keep in mind everything I just shared with you. I had invested three long years into those people and that area. I felt somewhat attached to it and them. None of that mattered to God.

He said, "I'm lifting this burden (to pray especially for those people and that area) from you now." Then I had a choice to make. Was I going to pray about it, or was I going to move? It took me a few minutes to collect myself and re-read His message, and I realized, *now means now*.

Then I put my Bible in its case, my watch on my wrist, my phone on my side and walked over to Mr. Potter. I interrupted his prayers and told him what the Lord had just said to me, and added, "It is over here for me; it's time to move on." He sensed the Spirit present and agreed it was time to leave, and we left. When the Lord spoke to me on that occasion, there was nothing to pray about. It was time to move, and I sensed immediately.

By leaving that day a chain of very positive events were triggered on my behalf and his too. I didn't ask what the next step was and could have cared less. All I know is that I passed some kind of obedience test. He has enlarged my territory and trusted me with more of His secrets since that day. You must move with your destiny when God says move to stay in His timing.

Many things that the Lord told me in the past, He didn't put dates on. Some took years to happen, and some haven't happened yet. This one was quick and I had to move to keep pace with destiny. I'm glad I did.

> IF WE'RE TO TRAVEL WITH GOD'S DESTINY
> FOR OUR LIVES, CHANGING THE WAY WE
> THINK WILL BE THE FIRST STEP.

If we're to travel with God's destiny for our lives, changing the way we think will be the first step. Hearing His voice must become a priority, not an option. Faith (concerning our destiny too) comes by hearing and hearing by the word of God; Romans 10:17. When we hear His voice, we must respond.

Reality is we should hear enough of our destiny to stay on track with it. When it's not mysterious, it's not difficult to follow.

Experience is a bloody good teacher if you have the time for it and friends at urgent care. But why not use some of the experiences you've just read about to help you move up river. You will encounter enough tests and trials along the way for sure. We have to be seaworthy, but we need to resist the urge to reinvent the sail.

God is too good to understand. What I've viewed as failure in the past was His idea for progress and promotion. We are guilty of wanting to hold that bird-in-the hand too tight, too often. Some lose good jobs to get better ones. Some lose positions to open businesses. It happened to me. Many call it luck, but I call it God. I have a Pastor friend that says "Nothing just happens." I agree.

> ### THERE WAS NO TIME FOR PRAYER, NOR ANY NEED FOR IT.

In chapter one, we targeted direction. We learned some vital info there, so now we will focus on movement.

And Elijah the Tishbite, of the inhabitants of Gilead, said to Ahab, "As the Lord God of Israel lives, before whom I stand, there shall not be dew nor rain these years, except at my word." Then the word of the Lord came to him, (the prophet Elijah) saying, "Get away from here and turn eastward, and hide by the Brook Cherith, which flows into the Jordan. And it will be that you shall drink from the brook, and I have commanded the ravens to feed you there."—1Kings 17:1-4

King Ahab of Israel was a wicked King and for his evil ways the prophet Elijah had called for a drought. It would punish him and the nation for his sinful ways, and help steer him toward God for relief and a changing of his ways, hopefully.

The Lord knew that King Ahab and his wicked wife Jezebel both wanted Elijah's head as the drought would surely come with a vengeance. He took immediate measures to protect Elijah.

"Get away from here! Turn eastward," God said. Sometimes you just got to pull up stakes and go. When God spoke to Elijah, he had to move quickly. There was no time for prayer, nor any need for it. He knew the will of God, and it was to move quickly.

Ahab and Jezebel wanted his head. This should speak volumes to us. Training our ears to hear the voice of God and obeying Him will often save our heads.

God will turn you away from most droughts if you are willing to hear and depart without questions. Some of us would have asked, "Why not wait till tomorrow; it's late. Or why not command a dove to bring me food?" I wonder how we would have fared many times if God had told us, "Get your own waiters!"

"But Lord those birds are loud," some would say. "They will tell on us with all that squawking." "Do you want quietness or food?" asks the Lord. "Forgive us Lord; we're on the way."

You not only need to move when God tells you to, you need to listen and go where He sends you. Did you notice in the last part of verse four that He had already commanded the ravens to feed Elijah *there*, and not somewhere else? If you aren't getting fed where you are, you might ask God if you're at the right place.

We often search and search for the complicated and completely miss the obvious. We've all been guilty, but we need to be getting a better handle on it. I've gotten hold of one truth that many conferences aren't teaching much about. A ten-point message on how to obey God isn't needed at my house anymore. You can give the CDs to somebody else.

I figure the one point that caused Jesus to work His first miracle will work just fine, and cause Him to work others too. Then I will not have to keep up with all those CDs either. Less is best when it works, and it was very productive at the wedding in Cana.

On the third day there was a wedding in Cana of Galilee, and the mother of Jesus was there. Now both Jesus and His disciples were invited to the wedding. And when they ran out of wine, the mother of Jesus said to Him, "They have no wine." —John 2:1-3

The Bible doesn't say who got married and it's not important. The weighty issue was that during the festivities of the wedding the wine ran out. Two or three factors could have contributed to this dilemma. More people could have come than anticipated, someone got their wine figures mixed up or the wine consumption was heavier than normal. I would lean to the latter reason. At any rate, the wine ran out.

> ALL SEEMED NORMAL UNTIL JESUS' MOTHER WENT STRAIGHT TO HIM WITH THE PROBLEM AS IF HE ALREADY HAD THE SOLUTION.

All seemed normal until Jesus' mother went straight to Him with the problem as if He already had the solution. Doesn't that puzzle you? The Bible clearly states that Jesus and His disciples were "invited" to the wedding. If you are invited to a wedding, you sure aren't hosting it! Why did Mary go to Jesus without hesitation?

Up to this time, there were no recorded miracles performed by Jesus in the Bible. He had been baptized by John, the Spirit had descended upon Him, He had added disciples and taught, but had not worked any miracles that we are aware of. John 2:11 even confirms this. When Mary said to Jesus "They have no wine (symbolic of revelation and truth)," was she insinuating that something much deeper than natural wine needed to be presented? I believe so.

If the real issue was natural wine only, doesn't it seem rather odd that the mother of Jesus didn't take her grievance to the bridegroom, his assistant or bartender? It was definitely an issue, but I believe Mary was speaking to her Son about a much greater issue. Surely even the servants knew where there were sufficient quantities of wine close by in Cana. Much thought and attention was given to having an abundance of wine at a Jewish wedding. To run out was quite an embarrassment, but it happened. Did it happen for a reason? Mary sure seemed to believe so!

The question is why? As we meditate on this scripture, more of God's intentions and timing come to light. The Bible states that Jesus' mother attended the wedding, but says absolutely nothing about her being a hostess either. But for some reason, an alarm went off inside her when the wine ran out, and she went straight to her Son with the problem. His answer to her was a bit cool.

Jesus said to her, "Woman what does your concern have to do with Me? My hour has not yet come."—John 2:4

"Woman what does your concern have to do with Me?" Jesus asked. It seems He was a little chafed by her statement, and look at how He answered His own question. "My hour has not yet come." What did that reply have to do with the wine running out that day? Absolutely nothing and everything!

> MARY HAD A KEEN EYE FOR THE PEOPLE,
> THE WINE, THE TIME AND HER SON'S HOUR.

If anybody on earth knew who Jesus was His mother did! She was the one that the Holy Spirit overshadowed and became pregnant by. She was the one that gave birth to Jesus without the help of a man. She witnessed the wise men bowing before Him with gifts. She heard the shepherds explain with excitement how an angel had appeared and told them the Messiah had been born in Bethlehem. He even told them where they could find Him and what He would be wearing and how a heavenly host then began praising God for Him. She knew who Jesus was!

She didn't know how everything was supposed to happen, but she knew that something should begin to happen. I believe she had that mother's intuition and had been praying and waiting and believed this could be the day for her Jesus to step into His miracle ministry.

Mary had a keen eye for the people, the wine, the time and her Son's hour. She somehow realized the season for bringing out the inferior wine was over and the time to bring forth His new wine was to begin. The guests didn't need more of the same, they needed a divine revelation of who her Son was. I believe she believed His hour had come!

I believe the shortage of wine was of great concern to Mary for she saw it as sign from God that He was ready to reveal His miracle working Son to the masses. She had waited over thirty years for this day to come, and Jesus knew exactly what she was inferring to. You can tell by His answer that He was taken back a bit by her implying it. He knew she was giving Him a motherly push, but He also knew the opposition that lay ahead. He was all man and all God, and was tempted in all ways like us. How could He be eager to face the cross?

Nonetheless, the wine (symbolic of revelation and truth) running out was the perfect invitation for Jesus to step forth and reveal how God had anointed Him with His power and word. A wedding, the joining of a man and a woman would be the perfect atmosphere to reveal to His bride-to-be who He really was.

When Mary told her Son, "They have no wine," she was telling Him, "They have no revelation of Who You are. Their wine (revelation) has run out. That season needs to be over. Give them the new wine (revelation of Who You are) and let a new season begin." She believed His hour (time) had come, and the wine running out was an open door. Why else would she address Him in such a way? Why else would He respond to her in such a way?

His response was in regards to His hour, the time He was to step into the fullness of His earthly ministry. He would then announce to the world by signs, wonders, miracles and words that He was none other than the Son of God. This would mark the beginning of His hour. It would also soon be the time for Him to tell the Jews that He was the Messiah they had been waiting for. His hour marked the beginning of a total committal. There could be no turning back once He stepped forth..

Man's wine had to run out before the Lord's best could be brought in. Mary believed the long awaited day she had prepared herself for, had arrived.

> ## MARY PULLED OUT ALL THE STOPS WHEN SHE SAID "WHATEVER HE SAYS TO YOU, DO IT."

Nevertheless, she knew Jesus would have to get the word from His Father in heaven before He proceeded. With the virtues of patience and faith supporting her actions she picked her way through the crowd to where the servants were gathered. She spoke one short command to them so as not to be misunderstood.

His mother said to the servants, "Whatever He says to you, do it." —John2:5

Were some of the servants on the same page with Mary? I believe so. How could she be so adamant and to the point with them if not? It seems to me that Jesus' mother and a number of the servants perceived something should happen now? Mary pulled out all the stops when she said "Whatever He says to you, do it." She meant it doesn't matter whether He says jump up or jump down. It doesn't matter whether He says laugh or frown. Don't go to the bridegroom, bartender, or tavern to see what they think. She told them to just do whatever He said.

Now there were set there six waterpots of stone, according to the manner of purification of the Jews, containing twenty or thirty gallons apiece. Jesus said to them (servants), "Fill the waterpots with water." And they filled them up to the brim.—John 2:6-7

"He wants us to fill those purification pots up. His mother told us to do whatever He said to do. Let's do it quickly! And remember, He said to fill them." The servants did just as He said to do. Then He instructed them further.

And He said to them, "Draw some out now, and take it to the master of the feast." And they (the servants) took it. When the master of the feast had tasted the water that was made wine, and did not know where it came from (but the servants who had drawn the water knew), the master of the feast called the bridegroom. And he said to him, "Every man at the beginning sets out the good wine, and when the guests have well drunk, then the inferior. You have kept the good wine until now!" John 2:8-10

Whether Mary knew for sure that Jesus' hour had come or whether she and the servants pushed the envelope a bit is not crystal clear and matters little. What is crystal clear is that either way she believed it enough to exercise her faith to the point that it caused Jesus to move into His hour and perform His first recorded miracle. Jesus proved her concern did have something to do with Him after all. One way or other, her concern and faith helped usher in His hour. The master of the feast attested to that! The good (best) wine was flowing now.

> # THE SERVANTS MOVED AND INVITED A MIRACLE.

And come to find out, Jesus was also concerned about our non-religious everyday needs like natural wine for weddings and such too. If you do the arithmetic, you'll find He miraculously turned about 150 gallons of water into about 150 gallons of fine wine. Does this give you a license to drink? No, this was a Jewish wedding and the order of the day, and it could last for many days. It was a festive occasion. There is so much more to tell about this wedding. A book is needed.

Back to the one point I was previously making, how did this miracle come about? By obeying one simple unusual command of Jesus, a miracle took place and the party went on. The command of Jesus' mother to the servants that day in Cana is the best one to obey to keep revelation flowing and our destinies moving? "Whatever He says for us to do, we just need to do it." I believe one of the main reasons we see so little of the miraculous is we do so little of what He says for us to do. The servants moved and invited a miracle. Mary practiced what she preached also. When she believed she had heard from God, she moved with it! She refused to cave in even when Jesus seemed reluctant to move.

Elijah sure didn't argue either when the Lord told him to get away from Samaria. He took off quickly and got his meals catered in by the ravens. When the brook dried up where he was sent, he moved on. God doesn't hold you to dried-up or dead things. If it's dry and smelly where you are, you need to ask God if it's time you moved.

Are You Ready to Ride

Jesus' mother told the servants when the wine ran out "Whatever He says, just do it." Nothing less, nothing more, just do it. It's nothing strategic. Nothing you planned. It may not sound normal. It doesn't take an engineer to figure it out. Just simple obedience is all it takes–be a servant.

Just take the Master's order and go fill it.

Too many look at the pots and ask, "Why?"

Don't reason yourself out of it,

 Don't let someone talk you out of it.

Don't pray yourself out of it, just do it.

If God said do it, it doesn't have to make sense to you!

If you want what God said is yours, go after it.

The ten spies were so concerned for their lives—they died.

If your gate is open, God is on the other side, go in!

Faith without movement is worthless. We are the most useful when we are on time.

God is no respecter of persons,
He will knock on your door.

A housewife can become a prophetess like Deborah.

One can be called from the desert like Moses to lead.

One can be called to build like Noah.

A mother can deliver children of destiny.

A prophet can be called out of nowhere like Elijah.

A rejected little brother can rise to power like Joseph.

A tax collector or bookkeeper can be used mightily.

A shepherd boy can become president like David.

A deacon or deaconess can be an evangelist like Phillip.

A young foreigner girl can become a Ruth.

Fishers can be called to be apostles.

God is looking for people willing to serve Him and move so He can elevate and anoint them to function in His real call on their lives. God has more in store for any that will move and roar.

Sons of God are led by Spirit of God. Sons and daughters will hear it and do it and move with destiny.

If you can't hear God well, dive into His word, and also hook up with people who can; let them help you improve your listening skills.

We all need to be wary about business, religiosity and indifference. All three have crept into our society and can severely hinder our ability to hear new revelation. It doesn't matter what the signs outside say. It matters what the Son inside says.

When Peter and the boys launched out and fished when and where Jesus told them to; they intersected with and harvested a miraculous catch. It broke their nets and created a new mindset about the directions, timing, and power of God's word.

Take the woman with the issue of blood. Life was flowing out of her through misfortune, and she said to herself, "I've got to get into that crowd." She had to move! She had to get out of that bed, get outta that sick place, and get outta that house. Tomorrow would be too late. Her Healer was passing by outside, and she had to push herself, ignore the crowd, ignore the religious law and make her way to Jesus or miss her opportunity. Healing was her destiny. She had been bleeding for twelve long years. If she hadn't moved, she would have died. The Bible says she was only getting worse, and the woman represents many in the church today. To me, she represents all those that haven't laid hold of Jesus yet as well.

I love to pray and pray much, but there are many things we already have God's will on that we just need to be doing.

God is trying to tell us something through reality TV. He is ready for His children to begin living in the reality of who we are, and understand more about where we are going. We will never know it all, and who wants to anyway? Our Lord is King of surprises. Heaven is full of them.

It's what He says that counts. The crowd is wearing Christian apparel but only playing the game.

Behind the barricade of pride is where many from destiny hide. When content to have it your way, severed from destiny you will stay.

The phrase "just do it" didn't originate in the 20th Century; it was about 30 A.D. and came from the mother of Jesus.

Ruth traveled with destiny through serving Naomi and her God. She didn't know what lay ahead, she just did it.

Just doing what He says for you to do—that is what will launch you into a position to deliver your destiny.

In 11Kings 7:3, we find four lepers with their backs against the outside walls of the city of Samaria. The city has been under siege by the Syrian army so long that people were starving to death inside. There was no common food in the city, and the lepers weren't allowed inside anyway. They were in a dilemma!

> ALL GOD WAS WAITING FOR WAS
> SOMEONE TO ALIGN WITH HIS
> PROPHETIC WORD AND MOVE.

Then they asked one another, "Why are we sitting here until we die? If we go in the city, we'll die. If we stay here, we'll die. Why don't we move towards the Syrians and surrender to them, and maybe they'll let us live." What a brilliant city saving idea the four outcasts came up with. All God was waiting for was someone to align with His prophetic word and move.

When the lepers arose and moved toward the Syrian army; I believe God dispatched one of His armies to go before them. The Bible says that God caused the enemy to hear the noise of chariots, horses, and a great army. Sounds like the host of heaven to me. It ignited so much fear in the overly sure Syrians, that they deserted their camp, left everything behind, and fled. The siege of Samaria ended and Israel was saved from what seemed to be certain defeat.

We don't hear much about the anointing to arise and move, but maybe the time has come when we should. The yoke of the siege was broken off of Israel when the lepers did it! Whether God sent His army before them, or He just orchestrated the sound of a massive army matters little. The yoke breaking truth is that human movement caused God to move! When He moved, it scared the wits out of the enemy. The whole Syrian army fled and left enough food, clothing, gold and horses behind that the stock market of Israel turned around in a day.

Sometimes movement is all that is needed from us for God to create a miracle. How many hours have we spent trying to figure out how to save our cities? It may only take movement. And evidently God isn't as choosy about who moves as we may think He is.

Principles and keys are great when you need them. But keys are useless when a door is open.

You must hear His voice and move with your destiny.

I have a pastor friend who says, "You may be on the right track, but if you sit there too long, you may get hit by a train."

Qualifications for delivering destinies are hearing from God and following His instructions.

What was one of the most important traits of all of the characters in this book? They were movers.

Having a destiny is one thing. Delivering it is another. Deliveries require movement. Just do it!

Chapter Seventeen

The Mountains Await You

When the rough fisherman Peter told Jesus that He didn't need to be associating with him, do you remember Jesus' response? He called Peter to be one of His disciples and later one of His 12 apostles. Those acts alone are proof enough that the Lord has a gift, call and position for everyone. No further evidence is needed, although the gospels attest to many more. Jesus is not interested in where you've been. He's interested in where you are going.

Every good gift and every perfect gift is from above, and comes down from the Father of lights, with whom there is no variation or shadow of turning.—James 1:17

God never changes and is no respecter of persons. He has good gifts and plans for you. Whether you are on a mountain, a valley, a sea or on the backside of nowhere; He sees you. Man may have overlooked you, but God hasn't. Nothing and no one escapes the eyes of the Lord. His eyes are searchlights. He hunts 24/7. It would pay all of us to memorize this previously mentioned scripture.

"For the eyes of the Lord run to and fro throughout the whole earth, to show Himself strong on behalf of those whose heart is loyal to Him..."—11 Chronicles 16:9

He is not looking for greatness. He's after the faithful. They will be the willing ones! He will take whoever fits in that category and prep them to show Himself strong on their behalf. This may sound like a tall order for many, but God has a tremendous amount of experience in this area.

The Sons of Thunder sure didn't have it all together when they left their boats by the Sea of Galilee that day. But anybody willing to leave their boat of ideas and follow Jesus has great potential. When we look in the mirror, we see a reflection, He sees a finished product. We see who we are; God sees who we will be. Too many are failing their bar exams, while God is saying, "Hey, it's all about My heart exam."

Many underestimate their position with God so doubt what they can accomplish for God. Nonetheless, the Bible informs us in Romans 8:16-17 that we are God's children, His hiers and joint heirs with His Son Jesus. That needs to be etched into our minds. When we are born again, God becomes our Father!

If we follow His orders, He can use us anywhere at any time. We have the powers of heaven backing us. He has plans for you. The only question is;— are you ready to accept them and move forward?

> WHEN YOU ALIGN WITH HIM, YOU
> STEP INTO ANOTHER DIMENSION.
> NOTHING STAYS THE SAME THEN.
> ALL THE DYNAMICS CHANGE.

As I've told you, I owned and managed an auto collision business for years, and the two most repetitious words I heard were, "We can't." Time and time again, we slashed the apostrophe and the *t* off and found "We Can." Then we just did it.

I can do all things through Christ who strengthens me.—Philippians 4:13

We haven't the strength or ability to carry out God's will in our lives alone. We must always work through Christ Jesus Who strengthens us. When we move away from our mirrors and behold the divine connection we have with Him, doubts lose their lease. They must vacate our premises.

Too many are folding their cards before they look at them in the light of God's word. Many of you may think it's about over, but like Moses, it may be just beginning. He thought he had missed his call until he turned aside that day. He made mistakes and had short-comings too, but God used him in a special way. And He is no respecter of persons.

They call the past the past because it's gone. Now is where the action is!

"It is the Spirit who gives life; the flesh profits nothing. The words that I speak to you are spirit, and they are life."—John 6:63

Jesus spoke these words to His disciples one day while in Capernaum. He wanted them to grasp what He desires us to grasp. We can't live the abundant life that He purchased for us, or accomplish His tasks with our natural abilities alone. We will fail every time. His Spirit gives the life that enables us to really live, and supplies us with the ability to achieve His will.

When we agree and engage with His call, His Spirit partners with us. He is our power source, and the more we depend on Him, the higher our confidence rises.

God is on our side, but we must become familiar with His voice to profit by His directions. Be willing to take the time to listen. Time spent with Him is time well spent. The longer you linger with the Lord the clearer His voice becomes. When you align with Him, you step into another dimension. Nothing stays the same then. All the dynamics change.

For instance Jesus found most of those He called into service unnoticed and working normal jobs (popularity will not put you over in the Kingdom of God). When those four fishermen and others said "yes" to what the Lord had for them, their lives and worlds changed drastically. When you hear God knocking on your door and let Him in, your house and future are in for a complete make-over.

I heard God knock on my door in my twenties and let Him in, and my world was transformed. After a few years He called me into His service, but like David and maybe you, I had some lions and bears to take care of first. His callings invite their conflict! Some attacked me from without and some from within, but with God's help, I silenced them. Their cronies continue to growl, but the sword of the Lord stills their prowl.

Refuse to let their roars frighten you away from your destiny during the in-between period. Be patient and allow God to train you wherever He chooses. It matters little where you get your degree, but through faith and patience we learn to see. It may be some out-of-the-way place, but if He led you there, stay until He leads you away!

More preparation time is needed for some callings, so you may see others leave before you. It will take faith and patience to keep your watch synchronized with God's and not somebody else's, but He's got your time. They don't!

Many of you are still in the prepping stages while some are already operating in that special assignment. Others are ready to take off now, but if God didn't reserve a seat on that plane for you, it's not going where you need to be. Delay is not defeat! It's waiting for the right flight.

> ## DELAY IS NOT DEFEAT! IT'S WAITING FOR THE RIGHT FLIGHT.

Some turn into where they think their destiny is waiting, but then realize it is only a pit stop and not the spot. God has provided these places for us to receive the fuel and resources we need to run our race. When it's time to leave, He will direct us out. Understanding everything isn't mandatory to keep our dreams alive, but pressing on is! Destinies are never found in our past.

As each one has received a gift, minister it to one another, as good stewards of the manifold grace of God.
— 1Peter 4:10

The vision of you *functioning in your gift* must be the fire that drives you on. It has a magnetic effect upon you too. Paul said in Philippians 3:12 that he had to *press on* to lay hold of that for which Christ Jesus laid hold of him for. Determination will turn ordinary faith into the high octane fuel needed to move beyond tests and trials, to grab hold of what God has for you. Those with attitudes that are violent in their pursuit of His call will bring heaven into earth. Kingdom business requires a kingdom mentality.

In the book of Revelation Jesus promises much to the overcomers, but warns the lukewarm. And Romans 8:37 says "Yet in all these things (trials, distress and persecutions) we are more than conquerors through Him (Jesus) who loved us." His victory over death secures the victory for us. It also denies our past failures to be considered or tag along and hound us. We more than just win through Him.

Your dreams weren't meant to mock you anyway. God wants you to live in the reality of them, and not just watch somebody else's on TV. You have that desire or you would have never picked up this book. Fulfilling the call of God on your life is an adventure you do not want to miss. Refuse to be average!

The heavenly verdict is "You have a destiny!" Be determined to live it and deliver it.

It doesn't matter which mountain (profession, position, or vocation) you're called to, you must be trained in His. Obtain your degree of Godly wisdom and patience, and then you can *reign* in any mountain He chooses.

The lions and bears are only tests. Like Goliath, they roar to distract you from God's best. With His strength you can overcome, and like David, your day will come.

You have a destiny! Your calling may get a little wild sometimes and I hope it does. Nevertheless it's not a mistake. You have divine appointments and contributions to make.

The Mountains await you. They are calling your name. Answer them with "I'm coming!" and let the fireworks begin. A willingness to be used strikes the match that lights the fuse.

About the Author

Maxwell Crapps is an ordained Minister and a front line prayer warrior. He graduated from Rhema Bible Training Center in 1985 and pastored for two years. He then founded, was President of and managed his own Collision Business, "Pro Body Shop," for twenty successful years. He faithfully served others until God called him into full time ministry in 2009.

He then founded Cut Thru Ministries, as God gifted him with the uncanny ability to cut through obstacles (whether race, religion, social or etc.) to help people rise up and embrace what God has for them today. He preaches the basics and the prophetic to enlarge and equip the 21st Century Church.

In September of 2012 while Max was in prayer at a Church he and his wife Lisa had only been attending several weeks, God spoke clearly to him. He said, "This is a good place for delivery." He meant "delivery" of his first book. Max knew the time had come to pull away from projects and give birth to purpose. What you are about to read or have just finished was what he went into the presence of God and came away with for his first book.

Much of what God reveals to Max is in poetic form and it is delivered through his messages and his pen. Thus the Lord led him to label this portion of his calling "Poetic Well."

For More Information

You can visit us on our website at:
www.poeticwell.com

You can also follow Max on his Facebook page: Poetic Well

Max is also a member of LinkedIn
For speaking engagements you can email us at:
maxwellcrapps@gmail.com
Or write to us at:
P. O. Box 1531
Thomasville, Georgia 31799

Whether you want to purchase bulk copies of
When Destinies Are Delivered
or buy another book for a friend, get it now at:
www.abooksmart.com.

If you have a book that you would like to publish,
contact Jon McHatton, Publisher, at A Book's Mind:
jon@abooksmind.com.

www.abooksmind.com

CPSIA information can be obtained at www.ICGtesting.com
Printed in the USA
LVOW13s1207101013

356209LV00002B/3/P